JOURNEY TO
UNKNOWN
INDIA

$7.50

JOURNEY TO UNKNOWN INDIA

WALTHER EIDLITZ

MANDALA
publishing group

Singapore   San Francisco   Mumbai

Mandala Publishing Group

1585-A Folsom Street
San Francisco California
USA 94103
Tel : 415.621. 2336 Fax : 415.626.1063

239C Joo Chiat Road
SINGAPORE, 427496
Tel: 65. 342. 3117   Fax: 65. 342. 3115

Centerpoint Bldg.
World Trade Center
Center 1, 30th floor
Cuffe Parade, Mumbai
INDIA, 400005
Fax: 91. 22. 218. 8175

Email: mandala@mandala.org
url: www.mandala.org

ISBN: 1–886069-22-0

Printed in China through Palace Press International.

CONTENTS

Foreword

Tales of personal spiritual journeys have always been and will always be interesting, if not compelling, reading. This is so because all of us, knowingly or unknowingly, are on a spiritual journey in search of ourselves. When we realize this and tread the path with awareness, the events in our life take on new meaning. Indeed, only then do our lives become truly meaningful.

Making the trek to the highest Himalayan peak involves passing through many foothills. In our progress, we will thus rise steadily despite many downward slopes. Only when we reach the top can we fully appreciate that without the lows, the highest peak would not be the wonder that it is. Walter Eidletz's sojourn, *Journey To Unknown India,* is no exception. As for low points, it would be difficult to think of more unfavorable circumstances out of which enlightenment might arise.

A Jew from Germany finds himself in an internment camp in India during the second World War. He had left his family in Germany and travelled to India in search of God. His wife loved him enough to honor his spiritual quest, the fruit of which he would share with her years later upon his return.

During his pilgrimage in the Himalayas, he was incarcerated and seemingly cut off from pursuing his ideal. Yet his passion for enlightenment could not be contained by barbed wire. Eidletz found his guru within the confines of the concentration camp. A dark-skinned, elderly Indian draped in robes donning a long white beard might have been what Eidletz was looking for with his outer eye, but his inner eye prevailed. His guru appeared to him with shaven head and white skin. Like Eidletz, he was from Germany, yet in their common homeland they might have been enemies due to Eidletz's Jewish heritage.

Much has been said in recent times about the "death of the guru." However, all philosophy and disappointing experiences aside, the endearing relationship between Eidletz and his guru is testimony to how meaningful and fulfilling the bond between a true guru and disciple is. In this world, it would be hard to find a more desirable relationship of mutual respect and love.

Eidletz's spiritual depth shines forth in his universal embrace of all that is spiritual, as he adopts and advocates his chosen path. His advocacy is unobtrusive, for it is heralded primarily through personal testament rather than dogma. Eidletz emerges from the myriad of India's spiritual paths on the *bhakti marg,* the path of devotion as taught by Sri Caitanya. He is not a *bhara bahi* Vaishnava or a devotee who carries the heavy load of external identification with his path's sectarian exterior. Such devotees do not experience their tradition. They remain only on its surface. Eidletz is a *saragarhi* Vaishnava or a devotee who experiences the essence of his tradition and can thus appreciate this essence whenever and wherever it appears, in whatever sectarian dress it may adopt.

Eidletz absorbed considerable knowledge from his preceptor and shares it with his readers. In doing so, he brings a discerning eye to the spiritual seeker, who all too often settles for the oversimplistic notion of what is spiritual. Eidletz's story is not burdened by metaphysical concerns as he speaks of the nature of spirituality. It is Eidletz himself, revealing his inner struggle and ultimately his triumph amidst the most awkward outer conditions, that the reader is drawn to. His personal testimony speaks loudly about a very lofty ideal in terms of its practical application in the life of a lay spiritual practitioner. Eidletz wrote this story more than 40 years ago, yet it remains fresh today and offers valuable insights to all who tread the spiritual path regardless of their particular sectarian orientation.

PART ONE
SREE

CHAPTER 1

JOURNEY TO THE EAST

The India-bound ship—Passengers of many races—Memories of the days preceding the war—The silent summons to India—Bombay—The search for Shri—A message from the Brahman

The ship that took me to India was an ordinary white steamer of the Lloyd Triestino Line. Now it lies somewhere at the bottom of the sea.

During the trip, I never felt the relaxation that I had always experienced when breathing the salt air of the open sea. In dining rooms and lounges, people crowded anxiously before the news broadcasts that told of changes in Germany's laws regarding the Jews, of new armaments or new speeches by those in power, who threatened war or remained hopeful for peace. Every plank, every white-enameled deck railing, every human body on board vibrated incessantly and rhythmically with the hum of the invisible engine, and in the same way, every heart quivered secretly in the face of its approaching destiny.

The passengers were divided into four classes according to the fares they could afford to pay. They were tucked into the ship's hundreds of small cubbyholes, each facing some unknown fate, and only the thin riveted walls of steel separated them from the sea.

The bombastic Italians who were on their way to the new empire of Abyssinia ordered wide-bellied, raffia-wound bottles of chianti with their meals. They gesticulated and talked excitedly and confidently. When the ship left Massawa they all disappeared, having remained in Africa. In what rifle-pits among the thickets of

3

the desert mountains are their bones bleaching now? In what prison camp did they succumb? How many of them survived the war and the turmoil that followed in its wake?

The quiet Jewish musician from Hungary escaping the terrors threatening his fatherland, who felt secure because of a contract that lay in his wallet, engaging him to play at a club in Penang on the Malay Peninsula—what became of him?

There was a medical student from the Philippines with his blonde, German wife. There were merchants and English officers on their way back to their posts in India or Burma. There were Indians, students and businessmen on their way home from America. A surgeon was returning to her native land after having been in London, as were members of a ritual dance troupe that had been touring America and Europe for two years. The red caste-mark on the foreheads of the women shone strangely as if some secret were hidden there. But in the evenings these women, too, danced jazz and the tango, tirelessly winding up the worn gramophone. The men played cards half the day in a suffocating smoking room.

Christian missionaries, Catholic priests in dark gowns with long, graying beards, walked among the Indians. They were on their way to the East to convert the people there to Christianity. One, a Frenchman on his way to China, paced the deck silently every day for a week with long strides, his gown flowing behind him. When he finally allowed himself to talk, he overflowed with repressed passion.

Two nuns stayed apart from the other passengers. They were holy sisters from Bayern, going to teach children in the Philippines. The handsome younger one looked like a bright angel, and the other, wrinkled and tiny, watched protectively over her companion.

My memory lingers among the many people on that ship, all those with whom I dined daily, brushed up against, spoke to, or only observed. What has become of them all? What fate has befallen them?

Around us the colors shifted, and the ocean altered its appearance. The hyacinth-blue sea once sailed by Odysseus beat against the sands of Egypt. I was a stranger in this world.

The Suez Canal appeared between endless dunes of yellowish-gray desert sand, which tumbled down the cement slopes of this artificial river bed. The ship carefully steered forward on the narrow, glittering blue waterway. Through the porthole, I could see far off into the desert.

The sea changed its name. A lighthouse stood in the middle of the Red Sea, above a naked yellow-brown cliff. Once again the endless surface of the sea stretched in every direction. At times we could discern mountains—those of the Sudan, peaks wrapped in the hot mists of Ethiopia, or the wildly rugged and fantastic formations of the Arabian coast.

After the Italians left the boat at Massawa, the Indian passengers began to stretch out on deck. They camped there day and night in their thin, light-colored garments. While the other passengers seemed to wilt in the stuffy, oppressive heat, they were full of life. Embracing couples leaned on the railings at night, over the roaring waves.

The electric fans purred continuously at top speed. Openings in the white ceiling pumped air, whistling, into the stuffy cabins. I held my head outside the open porthole, breathing in the warm night air, but it was not refreshing. Just below me water roared past the keel of the ship. The lamplight shone through the cabin windows like flames casting a white glow on the frothy, seething water. The sea lay black far into the night horizon; dark clouds gathered in the north. I walked up the softly vibrating steps to the captain's bridge and stretched out on a seat. Above me, the sky was filled with countless stars. The Milky Way looked strangely unfamiliar, its wide arc seeming to almost touch the surface of the water. I stayed on the empty deck the greater part of the night, as the ship plowed through the Indian Ocean. Listening to the noise of the waves, and looking up into the slowly revolving heaven of stars, I tried to relive in thought the confused events of those last days at home in Vienna.

I remembered the night when the mobs rolled in over the bridges of the Danube, and how the men raised clenched fists toward the houses and rhythmically shouted in chorus: "Death to Judah! Death to Judah!" I stood between my wife and my mother in one of the many dark windows, and we looked anxiously down at the shrieking masses. Fortunately, our little boy was already asleep.

In the middle of the room stood my packed trunks. My heart was heavy: at a time like this I was going to leave my wife, my child and my mother. And yet a voice within me commanded, "Go! Go! You must go to India! You must go!"

Now I lay on the captain's bridge in the warm breeze and looked up at the stars. Again I saw my goal before me: Kailas, the mountain of God's revelation, and at its base Manasarovar, the lake of the divine spirit. There, says the legend, the eternal human soul glides upon the clear waves like a swan, untouched by fear, hate, or desire.

The electric fans had stopped whirring and spreading what little cool air they could. The engines of the ship did not throb any longer. Passport officials were seated at the tables in the magnificent first-class dining room, and passengers filed past them in long lines. "What do you intend to do in India?" questioned a dark-skinned immigration officer, clad in a white uniform glittering with gold.

"I am going to study Indian religion and philosophy," I answered.

The officials eyed me with distrust and hesitatingly stamped my passport.

As I was shoved gradually nearer the exit, I happened to stand a moment beside the elder of the two nuns. "I can imagine how it must feel to be a refugee," she said slowly. "God help you."

Was I a refugee? I wondered in my surprise. I was headed for Kailas, I thought. But the mountain of revelation seemed to have sunk below the horizon.

The same unrest reigned in India as in all other places on earth. On the way to the hotel I drove past an alley crowded with loudly shrieking people. The chorus sank to a faint murmur, then rose once more. Despair and joy swelled up against each other like breakers at sea. "Are they lamenting over someone who is dead?" I asked the driver.

"No, this alley is the gold exchange," he explained. Wild, unrestrained cries of fear or delight accompanied each tiny swing of the exchange in silver and gold. India was no fairyland. India was a land full of selfishness, of the wild battle for bread, for money, and for gold.

Exhausted, I drove along one of the palm-lined streets of Bombay, feeling a breeze from the sea. Despite the beauty of the big city, I thought constantly of my wife, my child, and my mother. Would there be an airmail letter from home waiting for me in Bombay?

As soon as I had washed myself and stretched out a short while on the hard tourist bed in the bare room of the hospice, I hurried through the midday heat to the travel bureau of the American Express Company, where I had left my address.

I could have cried with disappointment. Nothing, not a word from home awaited me. The only letter for me bore an Indian stamp. Who could be writing me from India? I tore open the envelope indifferently. It was already several weeks old. An Indian lawyer informed me that Shri was in Hardwar and intended to undertake a long pilgrimage from there. If I wanted further information I should come to the lawyer's office some afternoon between three and six.

Shri Vishvanath Maharaj was the wise old Brahman to whom I had written from Vienna. I had wanted to accompany him on a pilgrimage to Lake Manasarovar in Tibet, but he had not answered.

I looked up Shri's lawyer immediately. The obliging official at the travel bureau pressed a guide on me despite my resistance. The office was situated in an old part of town where it was difficult to find one's way. He assured me that even if I took a car, the driver would never find the place.

The splendidly dressed man with a silk turban walked before me through the glowing heat of the sun. He remained on the sunny side of the street for the entire journey, avoiding the shade with painstaking care. As I went along the pavement I saw blood-red spots and puddles, and I wondered whether there had been an epidemic in Bombay. Later, I learned that the red spots had quite an innocent origin—betel-chewing Indians had been spitting in the streets.

My guide spared no pains in leading me entirely wrong. Triumphantly he marched me up one street and down another in the blinding heat, and at last he took me to the office of a lawyer. But, alas, it was the office of another, not the lawyer I was seeking. With a sigh, I paid the talkative, gaily dressed man and sent him away. I now went alone on my voyage of discovery. Dead tired, I stood at last in front of the house I sought. It lay on the same street as the travel bureau, Esplanade Road, exactly opposite the starting point of my wandering, barely thirty steps away.

The lawyer's office consisted of a single room, which was filled with busy clerks who came and went. A hushed, murmuring quiet reigned in the hall. A door opened noiselessly, and I entered the partition where the lawyer sat absorbed in his work at a desk covered with piles of papers.

The man turned his finely chiseled, tranquil countenance toward me and I became calm at once, though my heart still throbbed and perspiration streamed down my face. Through the open window, an invigorating breeze blew into the corner room.

With a searching look, his intelligent eyes rested on me. "So you are Walther Eidlitz? When did you arrive?"

"Today."

Two clerks came in with bundles of paper in their hands and stood waiting. But the lawyer had time for me. "And you wish to meet Shri?"

"Yes."

"Shri is no longer in Hardwar. Cholera has broken out among the pilgrims. I had a letter from Shri yesterday. He has gone farther into the mountains, to Nainital, which lies in the Himalayas at a height of over six thousand feet."

"In Nainital?" I cried in surprise. "Doesn't that lie on the pilgrim road that leads to Lake Manasarovar in Tibet?"

Walter Eidlitz
The Author

Sadananda
The teacher whom the author met in the Indian internment camp

Sri Krishna Chaitanya (1486-1534)
seated againts a tree, listening as his disciples recite the Bhagavatam.

Rana
Shri's first disciple

Shri Maharaj
the teacher the author met in the Himalayas

Prahbupada Srila Bhatktisiddhanta Sarsvati
Sadananda's Guru

Sadananda (shoulders covered with a dark cloth) (and the author in western dress) with the abbot of the bhakta-monestery Chaitanya math in Mayapur, the birthplace of Shri Krishna Chaitanya.

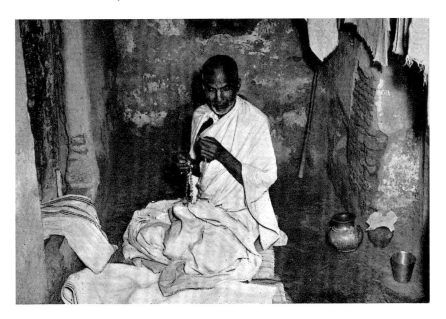

Adwaita Das Babaji Maharaj
a leading saint, philosopher and poet among the devotees of Shri Chaitanya, in his hermitage on the bank of Radha Kunda, chanting the names of God. The rosery that he holds has 108 beads made from the holy plant Tulasi. Advaita was an intimate friend of Sadananda.

The Temple of Chakleshvara
is situated at the foot of the holy mountain Govardhan. Chakleshvara is one of the four keepers of the holy land of Braja. after much persuasion the author was allowed to take for the first time a photograph of this temple, which dates back to pre-Christian times.

An Indian Sadhu
meditating on Krishna's Divine play and chants the holy names of god: Hare Krishna Hare Krishna Krishna Krishna Hare Hare Hare Rama hare Rama Rama Rama Hare Hare. He is sitting in front of his hermitage on a winter morning on the bank of the holy lake of Radha Kunda, the earthen ware pots and cloth on which he sitting, are his only property. The signs of the sect and the names of God are marked on the upper part of his body with earth from the holy ground. He speaks to no one but his single disciple, and this photograph was taken without his knowledge.

He nodded. "Yes, to the holy lake, Manasarovar. What do you intend to do first here in India?" he continued. "Do you plan to go to Benares? Or do you wish to meet Shri right away?"

"I wish to meet him at once."

The man smiled and sent for a telegram blank. He wrote: *Walther Eidlitz arrived today. Wishes to meet you immediately.* He gave the telegram to an errand boy. "Come here tomorrow at the same time, and the answer will surely be here."

The answer arrived punctually: *Send Walther Eidlitz here. Shri.*

CHAPTER II

SHRI

Farewell to Bombay—Tropical heat—Journey to Nainital—Shri and his disciples—A new life begins

Crowds of natives surrounded me. I was in a modern city of considerable size with street cars and double-decker buses. There were several hundred thousand brown people—light brown, olive brown, and blackish brown, young and old, in white cloths thin as gauze, but there was hardly one white face.

Meanwhile, electric advertisements flashed over bazaars, cinemas, and restaurants. America of today and ancient Asia contrasted strongly in this city. The people have remained Eastern. Their faces, their eyes and their brown hands are Eastern, and yet those hands steer the innumerable motor cars through the crowds. They squat on the streets; they sit in the dust in their white clothes; they crouch in various positions, often just as the meditating Buddha is generally pictured. Above them sway tall palms. Behind them, perhaps, is a Mohammedan hotel resembling a low shed, or a barber's stall where people sit crouched in the middle of the street masses, having their heads shaved. Only a small tuft of hair remains in the center of the crown, marking the place for Brahma's thousand-petal lotus flower, through which spiritually awakened souls leave the body at death. On the forehead, men and mostly women bear the carefully painted sign for the all-seeing spiritual eye.

For a few minutes I was drowned in Asia's seething multitudes. The big city of Bombay had vanished behind me. Gone were the electric advertisements, the arches of light, and the screaming caravans of cars. Around me now were only the quivering walls of the big, wide railway compartment and the sleeping gray figures on the benches. Outside, it was night.

For the first time I had made my own bed. I lay on my seat in the dark, gently rolling train. Through all the cracks in the car the tropical night pushed its way in. What a far-reaching country this was that I now traveled through for the first time!

The night stretched out and breathed hard on me. The next day would be merciless. On the ceiling, electric fans whirled in vain. The car was oppressively hot, and yet the compartment, the roof of which was sprayed with water at every stop, was cool in comparison with the air outside. All the shades were drawn and it was half-dim in the car. White light filtered in only through small cracks from the glowing skies and the naked earth, the endless burned-up plains covered by the express train hour after hour.

When I stepped out onto the railway platform at noon to go to the restaurant car, I was nearly felled by the white-hot hammer of heat. I should have come in November. May is the hottest month of the year in India.

Over bridges and wide rivers, over the Yamuna, over the Ganges, the train rolled on. Outside, the enormous country widened; the warm, damp tropical night came, and after it the glowing cloud of dust that was a new day. It could not be far now to the mountain in the north, to the Himalaya. But one could not see it.

I could not see it even when I rode in Shri Maharaj's car from Kathgodam through the burning heat up toward the foothills of Himalaya. Beside me slept Shri's old secretary, half-reclining and quite exhausted, recovering from a serious attack of dysentery.

I nearly grew dizzy on that road, which took me quickly, with numerous turns, up to a height of over 2,000 meters. Crowds of apes sat brooding on the stone barriers of the bridges. The air became cooler.

Now something flashed. We caught a glimpse of a lake between the green leaves of the trees on the other side of a mountain pass. Above the glittering mirror of water and the dry river beds that lay hidden in the mists of the plains, the houses of a many-colored Indian village arose, all with airy balconies. The village street swarmed with people. It led through a bazaar, up a steep hill, and was altogether too narrow for the car. We left the car down on the shore and climbed higher by foot.

Through the door of a hotel for natives came an old man with large, friendly eyes and a silver-gray beard. A golden brown sign was painted on his wide, furrowed forehead. It was *Shri*.

Something compelled me to bow reverently before this old man. I felt his hand—or was it the power in his blessing?—on my head.

A man of about forty, with a face like an Eastern knight in the legend of Parsifal, led me into a side room. It was Rana, Shri's disciple. I washed away the suffering of the last few weeks. I returned to Shri's half-lighted room; merely being in his presence made me cleaner and calmer.

Shri and Rana gave me oranges to eat. I ate at least a dozen of them one after the other. I felt unbelievably refreshed.

After a while, I saw a muscular, almost naked coolie loading my baggage like a tower on his head. Rana and I followed the coolie. The wind blew in from the lake, and Rana led me along the lovely green water to a house on the shore, a boarding house where Shri had arranged lodgings for me. There I was given vegetarian food prepared in European fashion. My new friends watched to see how I would react, for Shri had not always had pleasant experiences with European and American disciples. Not all of them had been able to adjust to Indian food and customs of living.

Rana appeared suddenly outside my door later that afternoon. "Shri is waiting," he called. "Come immediately."

We wandered along the edge of the lake together with Shri. He was silent, but at times I heard him murmuring "Hari Om, Hari Om." When we reached the temple of the goddess Naini, we met the old secretary. He threw himself down on the ground before Shri, touching his master's feet with his forehead as a crowd of Europeans and Indians watched. He left with Rana, the crowd dispersed, and I was left alone with Shri.

I opened my heart to him. I told him about my life, my work, my hopes, my fears, and my troubles. I laid before him all my faith and all my doubts. I told him also of my wife and child whom I had left behind, alone in a difficult situation. Not far from us was a bustling health resort, and all about us Indian nurses (*ayahs*) played with their pale European charges. None of this disturbed us.

A few days later, he said to me, "For a while yet I am not giving you the higher yoga practices. For the present I want to give you only *shanti*, only peace—divine peace!"

Is there anything greater than divine peace? I wondered.

Shri gave me peace—for a while. And he gave it not only to me, but to my wife as well, who lived thousands of miles away on the other side of the ocean, in an era and an atmosphere filled with danger. The first mantra of initiation that he gave me, he sent her also. He even gave her a new name. In the letters he sent her in response to my entreaty, he called her not Hella, but Shanti—Peace. He expressed the wish that divine peace should penetrate not only her, but bring strength and calm to all who came in contact with her.

Many who were near Hella during those days of confusion were surprised at Hella's—Shanti's—cheerfulness and firm confidence. Was it Shri's blessing that protected her?

CHAPTER III

THE FOUR STEPS OF MEDITATION

Jazz and temple bells—The legend of Lake Nainital—A reassuring dream—Rana, chief disciple of Shri—The silence of the Himalaya—First steps in meditation—Physical discomforts—Regulating the breathing—The power of the mantra—Meditation explained

When European eyes first beheld Lake Nainital about two hundred years ago, its basin was surrounded by fragrant virgin forest. The woods were filled with flowers, and wild animals wandered in large herds to the shores to drink. According to the Hindus, even the snake god had given his promise that a snake bite along these shores would not cause death.

I never saw a snake near Lake Nainital. Many of the wild animals have been driven away, and all that remains are the colorful birds that sway on the branches of the chestnut trees. Apes still reign over the steep cliffs of the south shore, and sometimes playfully push rock fragments down into the lake. In the thick forest of oaks and chestnuts, people have hewn out clearings and built country places, from simple bungalows to the stately residences of Indian princes and the English governor. A wide bridle-path circles the shore, and Western warehouses, schools, banks, and a large hockey field have been built. Near the shore is the graceful temple of the goddess Naini, and beneath its vault, naked Indian ascetics gather. But the temple stands in the shadow of an ugly European-style building that houses a cinema and a large roller-skating rink.

The jazz music from the cinema's sound system drowns the sound of the temple bells, which hang from a scaffolding and are often set ringing by believers.

Every evening I wandered along the shore with Shri Maharaj. "The holy rishis once lived on these wooded mountains," he told me. "Rishis are high spiritual beings, much higher than man. They have no earthly bodies, but it is said that they can assume human bodies if they wish. A thousand years ago, these rishis in human form were said to bathe every year in the Ganges. Later, when man's inner ear became closed, these ancient teachers of humanity drew themselves higher up into the mountains, into the regions of eternal snow."

"And where do they live in our days?" I asked.

The old man smiled. "In the snowy mountains about Lake Manasarovar."

The name Lake Manasarovar rang out over the water. The faraway lake in Tibet, my secret goal, appeared once again in a vision before me, enmeshed in legends, the heart of the world, the last bit of earthly Paradise. It is the source of four holy streams, to the south, west, north and east. The stream that runs southward bears with it sands of silver; that which flows westward bears gold; that which flows to the north bears emeralds; and that flowing to the east, diamonds. In some secret way, its waters fed the basin of the lake at the shore of which I now stood. Had my wandering led me right thus far?

The music from the cinema and the regimental band had died away. I listened to the tale of how Lake Nainital had come to be.

While wandering through the world in human forms, three of the seven holy rishis had come to these mountains. They had no water and were in great distress. Tortured by thirst, they prayed to Brahma, the Creator, for help. At his command they dug a deep hole in the earth, and the god allowed the living waters of faraway Lake Manasarovar to discharge into this deep basin. Then the lake was given the name Tririshisarovar, the lake of the three rishis.

A hockey match ended with loud acclaim from the crowds. The onlookers had dispersed. The musicians in red uniforms had packed away their instruments and returned to their quarters. The bells in the goddess Naini's temple rang out gently over the water.

I looked toward the west, where the sun was just sinking behind the wooded mountains. Shri Maharaj spoke further of the rishis and about a hymn they sang to the sun. The words of the hymn were not directed to the sun one sees with mortal eyes. It was a mantra to the spiritual sun, to that spiritual being hidden behind the sun we see. Shri sang first, and let me sing after him.

"Look deep into the blue heavens. Imbibe their depths so that they will give you strength," Shri advised me. We then read a few verses from the *Bhagavad-gita* together, a practice we continued every day thereafter. The old man interpreted the hidden, yet so apparent meaning in some of the verses. "It is the highest initiation book for all time and for all people," he exulted.

God himself speaks the *Bhagavad-gita*, the innermost God of which Brahma the Creator, Vishnu the Preserver, and Shiva the Destroyer are only aspects.

In the *Bhagavad-gita*, Krishna speaks thus to his friend Arjuna: "Just as a person casts off his worn-out clothes, so does the soul cast off the body and take on a new one. No one has the power to destroy the immortal soul."

The old man stood before me like a prophet of the spiritual sun. The waves of Lake Nainital lapped against the shore rhythmically, and I could almost see its sands once again, as in the past, thronged with wild animals seeking the water. At that moment, I joyfully realized that I really was in India, in Himalaya. Innumerable wise men and spiritual teachers had descended from those snow-covered mountains.

The next morning, shortly before waking, I had a dream. A ship bore me to a foreign land. I heard a voice: "Everything will turn out well for you. You will be reunited with your wife…. Give him the treasures, give them to him, step by step."

I arose happy at six o'clock. The street to the beach and the path along the lake were still empty. Only a few coolies trotted past with loads on their heads and shoulders. I waited for Rana.

By chance, I found out that Rana was a high-ranking police-man, commander of a district of several million inhabitants. He was Shri's most advanced disciple, and Shri Maharaj's private secretary spoke of Rana with the greatest respect: "In the evening when he is off duty, no one would believe that he is a member of the police. But if he should discover an error in the discharge of duty, he is said to be like a tiger. He is well-known as an excellent tiger shot: but he shoots no other game than this beast of prey."

Rana arrived punctually and climbed ahead of me. "Shortcut!" was the phrase I heard most often from him during the first few days. He always preferred time-saving shortcuts, taking the shortest way on these steep uphill paths through the thick forest of oaks and chestnut trees.

Looking far down between the tree trunks, one caught a glimpse of the lake, which lay lead-gray in the morning light. I waited in order to look—and to catch my breath. Back home in Vienna, I had run about a good deal, but I was not prepared for the quick climbing at this great height.

"It is only your legs that are tired, not your lungs," said Rana. We continued upward. I tried to follow his advice to forget my legs and succeeded. My breathing became one with the strong wind that blew through the world. My lungs were like the sails of a ship. The wind got hold of the sails and pushed the boat forward. I now climbed farther without difficulty.

"Shall we pause awhile?" asked Rana.

"No, we can continue," I cried and proceeded upward. A new person, an untiring wanderer, seemed to have entered my being.

Rana belonged to the warrior caste, an ancient nobility that he traced back through several hundred ancestors. "For a thousand years, time after time, they have fought against Islam," he said. I also learned later that Rana was a descendant of India's noblest lineage, the Sun Dynasty. He traced his lineage to Rama, the divine hero who in ancient times ruled India.

When we reached the top, Rana suggested: "Shall we remain silent?"

"Yes, let us."

In silence we sat beside each other on the jutting rock, and listened within our souls. We watched how the mists rose and sank, revealing a landscape of undulating woods and mountains. We looked toward the north, where at times one could get a suggestion of Himalaya's snowy ridges.

In silence we descended. When the way became less steep, and the rich foliage of fruit trees revealed the nearness of the lake, Rana began to talk about himself and his two little sons. He also spoke of his wife, with whom he had lived in a truly spiritual union and who now was dead. After a while he added, "I wish also once again to find the right wife."

"Don't forget that you must come to meditation with Shri Maharaj at ten o'clock," he called as we parted.

I went up to Shri's house somewhat shy and full of expectation. On the way I met young English men and women riding fine horses. They looked like young gods, these smiling youths, lifted high above the swarming masses of brown people. Most of them knew nothing of the soul of their Indian subjects. They remained strangers, even though they had lived in the country for thirty years.

I lingered in the hall of Shri's house to get used to the dim light. I rested awhile in Rana's room. I wanted to wash my hands and feet once again, although I had just bathed. Then I went barefoot into Shri's room.

Shri did not greet me in his usual manner, with a light, friendly gesture of the hand. The old man sat motionless on the floor, wrapped in a white mantle. Rana motioned for me to sit on the floor facing Shri. I did so. Rana, who also bore a white mantle, reverently threw himself before Shri and touched his forehead to the old man's bare feet. Then he lit a little stick of incense and placed it beside him in a candlestick. With whitish-gray ash from a glass bowl, he painted his sign on the crown of his head, his forehead, throat and breast. Now he sat motionless, his legs crossed under him and his back upright.

I felt Shri's gaze on me. "Look into my eyes. I am your friend," he said.

I looked at Shri. Mightier than ever, his wrinkled face surrounded by long black hair and a silver-gray beard, rose above the white linen garment that draped his figure. Mountains and chasms—whole worlds—were to be seen in that clear countenance. He sat there like cosmos itself, gray with age, yet resplendent with a quiet white-gold light which had become part of his being.

I did not meditate very much the first day. I was depressed, and I was not used to sitting with my legs crossed; it soon became unbearably tiresome. My limbs became stiff and cold, and ached. Ashamed, I got up and began to rub my numb feet. Shri arose and comforted me. He told me that for Europeans it was difficult at first. I must buy a straw mat and a deer hide in order to sit more comfortably. I must slowly learn the four steps to meditation: to sit, to breathe, to recite the mantra, and to sing it. To succeed, he explained, I had to develop the spiritual power within me from earlier existences on earth.

The sounds of the afternoon—the cries of merchants, coolies, and grooms, pierced the half-dim room. Sometimes a curious face peeped in through the window. Rana sat on the floor, reading aloud in an Indo-Aryan language. He read of Rama, conqueror of ten-headed demon Ravana, who had plunged "the three worlds"—heaven, earth, and hell—into slavery.

"Whenever justice is undermined and an excess of injustice reigns, I descend and appear among men. To restore justice, I am born on earth in every age," God promises in the *Bhagavad-gita*.

A hundred times and more, I sat opposite Shri in meditation. At those times I completely forgot my surroundings. I was always filled with the deepest emotion and reverence when I opened my eyes and saw the uplifted expression of the old man, silent and completely abandoned to the spiritual sun. He rose and painted the sign with cool sandalwood paste on my brow, my throat, and my breast, in order that my spiritual eyes might be opened.

Next time, I came to meditation with a straw mat of kusha grass, the skin of a deer, and a cloth under my arm. I seated myself without any cramps now, relaxed and comfortable. Now and then people came into the room and left again. The servant brought Shri's midday meal on a silver tray in silver bowls. This was the only meal the old man ate each day. I was surprised that all these activities did not disturb me in the least.

The deepest gratitude toward Shri welled up in me. Thus far I had had only a vague idea of what it meant to concentrate and meditate, and I still had a long way to go. But it began to dawn on me how meditation could develop.

Time after time I tried to concentrate during meditation, and often I saw majestic visions. But I had a secret feeling that this phase was only temptation—dangerous because it made one proud and conceited. This pride and all inner rubbish as well, all unrest, all spiritual uncleanliness, must first be carefully cleared away. One must work toward tranquility, as toward the shore of an unknown sea, and there on that shore one must wait until the divine world—if it so chooses—receives one.

When I rose from the floor after my attempt at meditation, my limbs usually ached for a long while. Yet I was marvelously refreshed, and the material world shone about me with a deeper radiance than before.

It is not enough to meditate temporarily or at a certain time of day. Shri often impressèd upon me this fact. "One must live in this spiritual atmosphere twenty-four hours a day," he said.

It would be several painful years before I could comprehend the four steps to meditation.

The first two steps of meditation, to sit and to breathe, are only preparatory, just as bathing and clean clothing are but outer preparations.

With practice, one is able to sit upright with crossed legs for several hours. The body does not interfere any longer. Even in pictures of a recently discovered ancient culture in the Indus valley, people are seen sitting and meditating in the same position that Indian yogis use today.

The art of regulating one's breathing has also been developed in India over thousands of years. When the breathing becomes calmer, the wandering spirit also becomes calm, for there exists a reciprocity between the current of breathing and the human spirit. But Indian scriptures point out that one cannot approach God simply by controlling one's breath; breathing exercises are only an aid. What is usually called yoga in Europe is the so-called hatha-yoga. Many people assert that by this method, one can preserve youth and health for an abnormally long time and acquire magic powers. The answer the great Buddha gave a yogi is well-known. The latter boasted that after twenty years of severe practice he had learned to walk on the water.

"What is the use of that?" said Buddha. "For a copper coin the ferryman will row you over the river."

"Do not waste time by practicing hatha-yoga," said my teacher Shri once. "You have already done that in a former existence on earth. Unknown powers can come to life within you, become a temptation, and hinder you on the Path."

The utterance of the mantra, on the contrary, lets in the important things. If one looks up the meaning of the word mantra in a Sanskrit dictionary, one finds the following attempts at translation: "Vedic hymn, holy prayer, formula for magic, secret, charm, lines of a prayer to a divinity, etc." But all these are only superficial meanings.

Many years after my first meeting with Shri, I asked another Indian guru, "What is a mantra?"

The surprisingly simple answer? "A mantra is something that creates loving devotion to God."

The Indian seeker of the truth, whether he chooses the path of action, wisdom or loving devotion, is convinced that the mantra he utters, and the divinity he thereby calls upon, are perfectly identical. Hence the reverence for the mantra, the importance of its being correctly spoken and the danger of its being misused for selfish purposes. Hindus have a greater respect for the spoken word than do people in the West. Not only every word in a mantra, but practically every sound and every word in the language is called *akshara* in Sanskrit, which means "the indestructible." *Akshara* is also a name for God.

A true mantra should be sung, not spoken. Indian scriptures call Brahma the Creator "the first singer." Our world is said to have sprung from the mantra he sang. The Indian initiate tries to awaken the divine sound with his entire soul, for it is the mantra of which all earthly sounds are only a shadow.

In the West, these ideas are probably utterly foreign, and yet there are traces of similar teachings. Time and again while in India I marvelled at the prologue of John the Evangelist: "In the beginning there was the word, and the word was with God, and the word was God.... Through this all things came to be.... "

MEDITATION

The first lesson is on food. Only easily digestible food should be eaten. Half of the stomach should be filled with solid food, one-fourth with water and the rest should be kept empty for movement or air.

The second lesson is on sleep. It must be regulated according to the age and health of each individual. One must not sleep too long or too little.

The third lesson is on the weather. It must not be too cold or too hot. One should be particularly careful during the change of seasons. Stormy and cyclonic weather are not good for meditation.

The fourth lesson concerns the location. It must be lonely and free from the presence of those who stand in the way of meditation. It would be well if no friends or relatives were present.

The fifth lesson is on the body. It should be kept restrained and healthy, away from those things that may cause the slightest stir, and away from the tumult of the multitudes.

The sixth lesson is on the mind. Generally there are three states of the mind: that of thinking on some worldly object of attachment or hatred; that of wandering from object to object; and that which tends toward lethargy and inactivity. None of these states are conducive to meditation. There should be a spirit of renunciation and a lack of thirst for worldly gain.

Certain means of livelihood are prescribed for the *sannyasis*. Even so, if any of these are found to stand in the way of meditation, they should be given up.

Yoga can be performed in the sitting posture. In India one chooses a place regarded as sacred and free from pollution, such as a river bank or a mountain cave. The place should not be too low or too high. First, a layer of deer or tiger skin should be placed over a mat of kusha grass, and over the first two should be a square of cloth. The whole is called *asana*. Each must have his own *asana*. Nobody else should be allowed to sit on it. It must not be moved from place to place, not even from one part of the room to another.

One must be very careful about the sitting posture. The legs should be folded. The whole spinal cord—the trunk, the neck, and the head—should be kept in a straight line. Failure to do this will cause diseases of the brain, heart, and kidneys. The meditator must be absolutely motionless. The eyes should be half-open and, though directed straight toward the end of the nose, should not be looking at anything in particular. The only way to do this is to try to look inward, or not to look at all. Now comes the most difficult part.

By practicing necessary things and avoiding unnecessary things, the wanderings of the mind should be stopped. Some can do it by force, but for the majority this is not possible. One must allow the mind to run, but keep a watch on it, always remembering the goal.

The object of meditation may be the personal God, his name, his attributes, his companions, his activities, or his place. Some meditate on the impersonal God. There are others who concentrate on the letter "AUM," which is regarded by the *Katha-Upanishad* as the last means of attaining the goal. In the opinion of the writer, all these practices are of equal efficacy, but the easiest and best course is chanting the name of God with love. Meditation will come. To those who favor meditation, the earnest command of the writer is this: Chant the name with love. It will give the desired result very quickly. This is also the view of the latest school of meditationists in India: the devotees of Krishna Chaitanya.

CHAPTER IV

VAMAN

Singing a mantra—The road to Almora—Story of Vaman, the Mighty Strider—Heat and thunderstorms—A picture of Krishna

The day before I left Nainital for Almora, I succeeded in singing a mantra to Shri's satisfaction. He burst out: "It is no longer Walther, but Vamandas. Hereafter your name shall be Vamandas, the servant of Vaman."

"Who is Vaman?" I asked. "When did he live?"

"Many thousand years ago," said Shri, and looked at me kindly. "Vaman was little in his outer form, but he conquered the three worlds."

During the following years of my stay in India, I was to become acquainted with the story of Vaman, the tale of his three mighty steps, and innumerably more tales about the doings of God. It was not only Shri Maharaj who narrated them for me, but also his most advanced disciple, Rana, and the Indian clerk Joshi, an office boy Shri had sent along to keep me company. These stories still live in the hearts of the Hindus, even simple farmers and coolies who have never learned to read or write. However, almost every narrator altered the stories somewhat. Like different strata of depth in the same endless ocean, the stories could suddenly assume new radiance and life, and their meaning became clearer when I read them later in the original text. It was as if they grew upward and yet downward, nearer to their source. This source was unfathomable God, He whom my friends called Krishna, from whose plenitude the divine saviors descended to earth. Vaman was one of the great saviors, one of God's Avatars.

I was now to be called Vamandas, the servant of Vaman, by Shri and Rana, and all the Hindus I met.

I sat beside the driver in the immense, rather worn Chevrolet bus from Nainital to Almora, and farther into Himalaya. The sacred word "AUM" was painted on the metal plate above the steering wheel. The peaceful trip down the many sinuous curves of the country road wound its way over deep crevices and through burned-up fields.

The bus stopped suddenly. Long columns of cars blocked the road. Two buses had collided, and one driver was seriously injured. Nobody ventured near the wreckage. It was only a quarter to ten in the morning, but it was rumored that we would have to wait until two o'clock in the afternoon before the police could arrive and make their report.

I was surprised at myself for not being in the least impatient. The queues in both directions grew longer and longer. Men, women, children, and pilgrims from all parts of India gathered on the walls, along the side of the road, in the dust of the ground and on the mountain slope. I wandered to and fro on the road with Joshi. While we waited for the police, he related the story of Vaman.

In olden times, God had descended upon earth in the form of the Brahman boy Vaman. At that time, the powerful demon king Bali ruled the earth, the underworld and heaven. The Brahman boy shyly begged Bali to grant him a wish. Although the high priest of the demons warned him, proud Bali sanctioned his request in advance. The boy then asked for as much land as he could cover in three steps.

Vaman took his first step.

Surprised and frightened, the king and his court watched the little boy grow until he reached the clouds. There was not a grain of sand in Bali's immeasurable kingdom, on the whole of the earth and on all the starry worlds, not covered by the foot of the mighty strider.

Vaman took the second step. Bali, his eyes opened to spiritual vision, saw that Vaman had covered the visible world, future worlds, and heaven.

Vaman's voice rumbled from the clouds like thunder. "Where can I set my third step, Bali?"

Trembling, Bali stammered: "Place your foot on my head!"

The ignorant man did not yet know that even his head was not his own, that it too belonged to God. Vaman placed his foot on Bali's head. The touch of God's all-hallowing foot took from him not only his power and his desire for power, it also took his wickedness and ignorance. Bali was redeemed. With overflowing love, he washed the feet of God with his tears.

"A drop of the water that had touched the feet of God fell into our world, and became the River Ganges, which flows through all of India. For thousands of years, the demon Bali has been glorified in India as one of the beloved friends of God," ended Joshi.

The rivers and streams in the deep valleys, seen in the midday haze that enveloped the Indian plains, suddenly assumed a new radiance. They were all tributaries of the Ganges.

The crowd of people on the road had awakened to action. Someone had hit upon the idea of digging into the gravel slope on the side of the road, which gradually became wider. A little car slyly slipped past, and a cry went up from the crowd. All hurried back to their cars, and while a few dozen people continued to dig and shovel, even the bulky buses got into motion. We drove farther north, up into the mountains, without waiting for the police.

A breeze fanned my hot face, and with joy I felt the coolness coming from the forest.

We had climbed from a narrow, wooded valley to an open area. I looked around me at the land. In terraces, in wild streams, in groves of silver oaks and trees with red and violet flowers, the land sloped down toward a river. Rice and wheat grew in the depths just above the boulders on the riverbed. Down on the shore, under a high cliff, one could see a mahatma's old hut.

The bus stopped for a moment with creaking brakes. The driver hopped out to pick a couple of flowering branches from a holy shrub and we were on our way. We traveled farther in a close column. At one place, the river widened, and we saw buffaloes in the water. Trees mightier than any I'd seen before arched over thatched-roof huts. Pilgrims came toward us, many of them half-naked: they were returning from the source of the Ganges. One pilgrim in an orange-colored mantle waved to us. I waved back. I was one of them, on a pilgrimage just as they were. It made me so happy that this land had received me with open arms.

"During the rainy period, all of these nearly dried-up streams are filled with water," said my companion. "All the yellow-brown mountain terraces become green."

Shortly afterward, the air shook with a heavy thunderclap and the sun disappeared. Water poured from the skies in lashing streams, too strong for the tent covering we tried hurriedly to roll out. Thoroughly soaked, we sat there as lightning struck right beside us and thunder boomed in the forests.

"The rainy season has come too early," whispered a passenger.

The bus slid forward on the flooded road into a wood filled with gray mist. Shri's private secretary pressed a picture protectively to his breast. It was a picture of Krishna as a smiling boy, embraced by the sacred syllable AUM. The curve of the Sanskrit character hints at innumerable unborn worlds, for Hindus believe this divine word is the source and preserver of everything. When the world comes to an end, all shall again return to the AUM, in which God dwells.

The dried-up land drank from the life-giving flow of water.

CHAPTER V

SWAMI NITYANAND

Almora the mountain city—A letter of admonition from Shri—Swami Nityanand—His modern ambitions—Life in the pilgrim shelter

The city of Almora lies high up on the narrow ridge of a mountain. There is a majestic panorama on both sides, down over the yellow-gray landscape of terraces and away toward the wall of mountains on the horizon. But the true mountain giants are usually hidden.

Almora was for a many years the capital of the independent kingdom of Kumaon. More than a hundred years ago, the English stormed the mountain city, and now the Court of Justice reigns in the former royal castle, high up on a cliff.

The hotel in Almora had a fine name, high prices, and bugs. Like the newcomer and inexperienced traveler that I was, I complained about the bugs, and more mats were laid upon the floor. But Rana came to the rescue, and, in answer to his polite military request, the bug-infested mats were aired in the sun for a whole day. After that, the situation was somewhat better.

Outside our row of rooms was a terrace with a lovely view of the sloping rock projections with their numerous ledges. When the sky was clear, one could see the highest Himalayan peaks to the north. My room faced this direction, but just outside was the place devoted to the daily needs of human beings. The barrel system! Instead of loving humanity, I began to hate parts of it. Instead of rejoicing at the colorful crowd which filled the open

29

place outside the hotel, I suffered because of all the penetrating noises and smells that filled the house day and night. It was a trial that I endured very poorly in the beginning.

To my surprise, Shri Maharaj retained his happy disposition even in that house. He did not seem to notice the blaring musical ensemble outside the hotel encouraging passerbys to visit cinemas or buy some European medicine. Shri appeared not to observe anything at all, but he could immediately detect bad thoughts in my mind. He would look at me silently, slowly shaking his head, and that was worse than punishment. In spite of the surroundings, his room had become a quiet, luminous sanctuary. It brought me indescribable happiness to meditate in his presence.

Thus I took the first steps toward a completely Indian environment. In Nainital, according to Shri's wish, I had still lived in European fashion in the boarding house; the only change was that I had given up eating meat. It was a long, long time, however, before I learned to like the decidedly different Indian food that Shri's cook prepared for us in the hotel in Almora.

One evening Shri's secretary handed me a letter. Shri's son-in-law, who was visiting me, laughed. "Shri sends me a similar letter every time he is dissatisfied with me," he said.

The missive contained simple, affectionate advice for my mode of living:

"Regulate your meals carefully. Eat rice only once a day. Eat only a little in the evenings.

"Learn to lead a simple life, and a clean one."

"It is not so important to go to Lake Manasarovar and Mt. Kailas. The true Kailas lies within you. It is this you must seek to attain."

These admonitions helped me, but it was very difficult to take to heart the words about Lake Manasarovar and Mt. Kailas. Rana had also reproached me many times. "Your guru is here, the true spiritual teacher. The spiritual treasures you seek are here. Is it not meaningless to leave him in order to rush farther up into the mountains? Be patient."

Shri, Rana, and I sat deep in meditation on the carpet covering the floor. I had just gone through a difficult hour. I had convinced myself to refrain from making the long pilgrimage to Kailas and Lake Manasarovar this year. I had finally realized that Shri was right. Physically, I was not ready for the difficult excursion; above all, I was not mature spiritually. I had much to learn.

Just then a stranger entered the room. He was almost naked, and his long, grayish-brown hair was powdered with ashes and gathered in a topknot on the crown of his head. His strikingly light-skinned body was as straight and muscular as that of a youth—although I learned later that he was sixty-five years old. He wore only a narrow, orange-colored cloth about his loins. On his shoulders hung a tiger skin, and he carried a wooden scepter. After greeting Shri and Rana, he embraced me.

To my utmost astonishment, he immediately said, "Without doubt you are coming to Kailas. I promise you that this year you will come there and to Lake Manasarovar. You are going along with me!"

His name was Swami Nityanand Sarasvati, and he was president of the committee for the furtherance of the ancient pilgrimages to Mt. Kailas and Lake Manasarovar. He told me that he had recently been elected as the spiritual leader of more than a hundred million Hindus. At the Kumbha Mela festival in Hardwar, where more than a million pilgrims gather once every twelve years, he had been found worthy to rule north India and had ascended the throne accompanied by all manifestations of honor.

This spiritual and religious kingdom had lacked a leader for two hundred years because no one had been deemed worthy of the throne. He had been found worthy, he asserted, and in answer to my questions related the following.

Shri Adi Shankaracharya, the reviver of Hinduism during the Middle Ages, established religious strongholds in the north, south, east, and west of India. The leader of each exercised spiritual jurisdiction over a fourth of the immense realm of India. The Himalayan town of Jyotirmath was the seat of the northern jurisdiction, which included Kashmir, Nepal, Kabul, Mt. Kailas, Lake Manasarovar, and several Indian provinces.

An official Sanskrit document summed up the honors and rights now granted Swami Nityanand:

> The Great Holy of Holies, who rules all spheres of spiritual life; who is a great yogi far along the Path, with the power to interpret, expound, and perform initiation; who knows all the religious texts; who has been given the power to chastise the four Vedic castes—the Brahmans, Kshatriyas, Vaishyas, and Shudras; who has supervision over all ascetics; who has unrestricted power to apply the rules and laws in the religious and social lives of all disciples, and whose supervision and recognition is demanded before the rulers of the civil states in this territory may ascend their thrones; he who is the spiritual leader over hundreds of millions of Hindus—he has ascended the throne in this realm of the north, in order to administer the social and religious laws there with unrestricted power....

This man was very eager for me to undertake the pilgrimage to Lake Manasarovar with him this year. "Later on I shall be inaccessible," he said. "I shall travel about constantly surrounded by strict ceremonials requiring a pledge of silence and accompanied by torches and a servant."

I was to undertake the excursion in the orange-colored mantle worn by pilgrims. Nityanand expressed the wish that I should move into the pilgrims' quarter, which we immediately visited. "It will do you good to live among the ascetics. It will cleanse your soul," he said. He wanted me to move right in, but Shri protested mildly.

Nityanand was a dictator. He came from southern India, and spoke English much more fluently than Hindi. His features reminded one more of a Russian than an Indian. Night and day, summer and winter, he was dressed in his thin orange-colored loin cloth, a tiger skin over his shoulders, but otherwise naked—even while wandering high up in the mountains. He wore the same dress when he visited the English viceroy and the ministers and maharajas he included among his friends.

At one time, Nityanand had lived quite another kind of life. He had been a famous young lawyer with a large practice, then governor over three combined Indian districts as large as many European kingdoms. He was a very powerful man when he met his guru and suddenly decided to give up everything—wife, children, income, position, and power—to withdraw into a rock cave and become an ascetic. He told me that while in isolation he received a command from God to take charge of the endless difficulties connected with the pilgrimages to Lake Manasarovar and Mt. Kailas.

While we squatted on the ground around him, Nityanand and Shri worked out his plans. He was going to introduce electricity and hygiene into the cloisters of the lamas in Tibet. He wanted to build half a dozen pilgrim shelters along the way. He weighed and rejected the possibility of a connection by air: Although the smooth plateaus of Tibet were excellent landing places, storms and mountain ridges would make landings too difficult. I almost shuddered when he exclaimed emphatically, "No one is going to die on this pilgrimage!" And he added: "I shall never give up."

To the great interest of the population of Almora, I drove that afternoon with Shri Maharaj and Swami Nityanand to the pilgrims' quarters. A narrow, winding road went over the steep slopes, deep into the blooming forest. The last part of the way consisted of climbing a long flight of stone steps. Upon the terrace stood about a dozen pilgrims, their faces, necks and arms gaily painted with colored ash. They greeted us by singing in chorus ceremoniously:

AUM AUM AUM
Hare Krishna Hare Krishna…
Hare Rama Hare Rama…

With astonishing potency, the names of God and the sacred word AUM echoed over mountain and valley, through the forests and in our hearts, as we climbed the steps. In the sound A, the song rose and the tone hovered, until in U it swelled out in full force, and at last in M it slowly died away into silence.

The song—its words, its melody, and its secret—fascinated me.

Twilight fell. The peaceful AUM of the chorus still echoed about us from above. I drove back with Shri to Almora through the blackness of the night forest. I packed my belongings by candlelight at the hotel. The next day, Shri himself led me to the pilgrims' quarters, a large, beautiful bungalow with pillared halls on all sides that had been remodeled as an ashram. I was given a room to myself. It had two windows and a glass door. "Throw out all the chairs except for one or two!" Shri advised me. I did so. Now the furniture consisted mainly of a table and a very dirty carpet on the floor.

I found out that Shri intended to go away in a few days and perhaps not return for several weeks. When my teacher had left me and the evening breeze murmured in the tree tops around the strange house, I knew this much: For the first time I was absolutely alone.

CHAPTER VI

DIARY FROM THE HIMALAYAS

Singing hymns to Shiva—The Tamil from southern India—Story about Gandhi—AUM, the mystic syllable—Simple diet—Preparations for departure—An attack of dysentery—Shri returns

On the first evening in the pilgrim's quarters, from eight to nine o'clock, I sat on the stone floor with the other pilgrims on my mat of kusha grass. The only illumination was a small kerosene lamp. Swamis sat close beside one another along the walls. Only one had placed himself in the center of the room, a man with dark, fanatical eyes. The others shook and shoved him to get him to move. He took no notice. He had fallen immediately into a deep trance. At times it seemed as if he were looking piercingly at me with his distorted, staring eyes, but as a matter of fact he was far away.

For more than an hour we sang hymns to Shiva, who destroys earthly things and frees the spirit. One after another, the pilgrims and ascetics eagerly took up new lines. A wave beat upon the shore. And then a new one, one after another, hundreds of them.

This was no duty-bound prayer. It was a song filled with joy, conscious of power. Just as a Western athlete enjoys testing the strength of his well-developed body, these swamis test the strength of the soul.

At first, there was only shy conversation between myself and the slender, almost beardless Tamil who was to look after me. His name was Nishabodh and he was a formerly a bookstore clerk in Madras. When I asked him if he had any parents or relatives, he was painfully upset. He did not seem to know if they were alive.

35

SHRI

Since a swami must leave his home, parents, and everything that binds him to the material world—eventually, he must forget even his own body—Nishabodh decided to move to north India. He had lived five years in Rishikesh, another valley in Himalaya, as a disciple of his guru, and now he wanted to go to Kailas. He was young, not more than twenty-five years old, and a bit of a fanatic.

I awakened refreshed at five-thirty in the morning. A gentle rain fell. Clouds hung heavily over the precipices of the Himalayas.

I made my bed—that is, I hung up the quilt I had laid on, as well as the one I spread over me in the corridor of pillars. There were no bugs; otherwise they would have come in armies. Obviously bugs and war in the trenches have something in common: Only the new-comers get caught.

Nishabodh taught me not to lie too near the walls. He was appalled at the thought of killing a bug and was convinced that if he did so he would be reborn as one of these unpleasant insects. When I asked Shri about this, he had quite a different view. "Go ahead and kill them," he said. "If you throw them out, they will return and bother the other swamis. Bugs have a miserable existence." But Rana explained thus: "It is well that the bugs wake you at night. They are reminding you that you really ought to be meditating."

Nishabodh told me a story worth repeating about Mahatma Gandhi. Gandhi had opened an ashram of his own, and people came to him so that he could teach them yoga. But instead of the exalted yoga practices they expected, they received instructions to begin by cleaning the latrines. When they refused, or if someone became ill, he performed the job himself, for yoga is service. Nishabodh's guru once said to him, "If one has become a yogi of renown, one must yet be constantly prepared, even in the midst of disciples or followers, to carry a trunk on one's head and take it to the railway station, without out a trace of false humility. If one cannot do this, one is not a true yogi." Young Nishabodh lived according to these teachings. I often

36

think that this thin, ugly person, who cheerfully helped me, had become an angel of light by means of yoga.

I sat in my room in the deep peacefulness that follows meditation. I looked down upon the quiet, sunny terraces on the other side of the valley, where the village of Kalamati lies.

I wandered in the clear morning sunlight into the valley. From a distance, I could see the sharp contours of a pointed, dark gray cupola, which ends in an upright lingam stone, the symbol for cosmic creative power. On coming nearer, I could see that it was an old temple of Shiva. Just outside the entrance stood a mighty tree that had recently been split and charred by lightning.

Above and below the temple were immense stone basins filled with water. In the upper basin, two naked dark-brown men who had just lathered themselves with soap began to rinse off. I removed my shoes and socks and washed my hands and feet. One of the men kindly moved his copper bowl from the spouting water so that I could get near enough to wash myself.

I went barefoot to the threshold of the temple, which was gray with age, its roof ready to cave in. I bowed deeply and reverently. The men in orange-colored mantles nodded their approval.

Now I knew where they went daily when they left the pilgrim shelter with their copper and bronze bowls. Although an excellent spring gushed forth nearby, these men fetched water and bathed at the temple of Shiva.

Shiva the Destroyer is the god of yogis, and death and resurrection. A thin stream of living water drops on his head where he sits, lost in meditation.

I have been told that those who choose to serve Rama must first pay homage to Shiva for three or six months. Rama, Krishna, Narayana, Brahma, Vishnu, Shiva, Vaman—these are all different aspects and names of the one Almighty God.

There was nothing but green slime in the large square stone pool below the temple. Clean and clear water came from only one place. A man was standing there on the damp ground, drinking out of a bowl. He motioned for me to sit down. In front of the pool were aisles of fallen pillars. Small square huts topped with lingam stones were scattered about.

Around the temple, the somber green mountain slopes spread severely and majestically into a wide round bowl. I sat on the lawn in the midst of cow droppings as if in a field in the Alps. When I turned my head, I could see the land slant downward in grassy slopes, in depressions traversed by goat paths. In the depths was a wooded world.

Dark gray banks of clouds hovered over the mountains in the west. On the flag stones in front of the temple, a demon animal, hewn in dark stone, stood praying in the midst of grazing horses and cows. A similar figure stood on the sloping moss-grown pyramid of the roof.

A wide, curving road stretched high over the deep ravines from the temple to the pilgrim shelter. The gradual shifting of the ground over hundreds of years had dislocated the narrow stratified cobblestones and the large flat stone blocks that made up the road. It was often necessary to hop from one stone block to another.

The pilgrims greeted me with a friendly "AUM" on their way to the temple water to take a bath, just as Nishabodh would wake me with "AUM" in the morning.

From the syllable AUM, it is said, all the languages and all the books of Veda have sprung. The Vedas are leaves of a tree which has its roots in heaven and grows downwards.

The rainy season began in earnest. Each time thunderclaps accompanied flashes from the heavens, I thought the lightning had struck one of the ashram buildings. But half an hour later peace reigned, the rain ceased, and the earth swallowed all the water.

The pledge of silence that Shri Maharaj imposed upon me before his departure gave me great happiness. I was not to utter a word before noon. If I needed something, I would inform the pilgrims in writing. There exists a mighty force in silencing one's inner self, the soul, and not just the tongue.

Nishabodh and I made a strange pair. His native tongue was Tamil, mine is German, and we conversed in English, which neither of us spoke very well. He cheerfully tried to teach me whatever little Hindustani he picked up in the market square and in the bazaars. At night, he impetuously studied a Hindustani grammar book found among my belongings, and then he would come triumphantly with the new rules he had just learned. Nishabodh was very surprised that I neither smoke nor drink, and that it was so easy for me to give up eating meat. But the simple ashram food was so strongly spiced that it burned one's tongue. We ate rice, vegetables, and Indian bread, which is thin as a leaf, at eleven in the morning, and a little bowl of vegetables and bread at ten in the evening. Most of the Indian ashrams serve only one meal a day. In the light of a glaring kerosene lamp, the pilgrims sat outside in the evenings in a long row, waiting for their food, while flowers around them gave off an overpowering scent. People from all parts of India, from all castes and conditions, gathered there. All of them had cut themselves off from their pasts and given up everything they owned in order to become sadhus. But not all of them had succeeded in completely forgetting caste distinctions, although it is a requirement. Sometimes, through the walls of my sleeping room, I could hear long and frequently bitter discussions that continued until the late hours of the night. They would get worked up over the provisions in regard to meals. Even Nishabodh could talk about that for hours at a time.

New pilgrims joined us daily. They filled every spot of the floor in the ashram. Nearly a hundred lived in the pilgrims' shelter, and many others were housed in the various buildings in the town. Even at night they would come knocking on the glass doors, asking to be let in. The news had spread throughout India like wildfire that the committee provided all expenses, equipment, food, and lodging on the long pilgrimage. Many were real seekers of the truth, while others perhaps only wore the orange mantle of the monks. They divided themselves into groups. Services were held in both the lower and upper stories of the house. From above and from about, hymns to

Shiva drifted in to me in the evening. Almost all night, people were busy packing chests, sorting equipment in the pillar alley outside my window. Coolies sat squatting on the floor, waiting.

The undertaking was enormous. The nearest railway station was 120 kilometers from Almora. The pilgrimage, coming and going, was about 950 kilometers long and went through passes that were 6,000 meters high. There was no country road. Every kerosene lamp, every sack of rice, had to be borne on somebody's back. There seemed to be a shortage of money, because more pilgrims had arrived than were expected. Swami Nityanand had gone to Delhi and Karachi, tiger skin on his shoulders, to get donations from rich merchants. But India, too, felt the economic crisis. Nityanand returned, ill and troubled, his mission unaccomplished. For the first time in his life, he had a fever. But his motto was, "I shall never give up." The next day, despite his illness, he made the two-day trip to Bombay to collect money for the pilgrimage.

In the shelter, we lived like a big family, troublesome and full of dissension. New wanderers came daily and lodged with us. The spacious attic was already full of pilgrims who were headed for Manasarovar and Mt. Kailas. One of them, a powerful old man with a white goatee, took me under his wing. At one time he had been a machine engineer in Europe. He told me that in his youth he built thousands of diesel motors in Stockholm. Now he owned nothing but a book, a commentary to the *Bhagavad-gita* by Shankaracharya. When he saw that I was interested in it, he wanted to give it to me right away, so much so that I had difficulty in preventing him from doing so. When I got a hole in one of my sandals, he and Nishabodh accompanied me protectively to Almora, so that in my inexperience I would not be cheated there. The shoemaker asked only two annas, about two cents, but both of my protectors disdainfully turned their backs on this covetous person, and dragged me away, discussing eagerly. It was too expensive. Another shoemaker asked only *one* anna, and that was still too much. We wandered up and down the streets, through poorer and poorer quarters, until a shoemaker mended the hole for half an anna while I stood barefoot beside him. My companions were as happy as if they had won a victorious battle. We returned through the flowering bushes on the hillsides to the pilgrim shelter.

I became ill with dysentery. The water in Almora has a bad reputation. Nishabodh tried to cure me with medicine he had with him. My eyes were inflamed, too; I must have gotten some strong acid in them. For three days I was nearly blind. Outside, the rain fell incessantly. When would Shri come back?

Shri finally returned a few days earlier than intended because he felt that I needed him. I still spent my nights in the overcrowded pilgrim shelter, but all day long I was with Shri in the little house in the forest, which he called Anandakutir, "the hut of blessedness." A Brahman in Almora was suddenly inspired to place his house at Shri's disposal as long as he lived. My eyes healed. Shri told me in all seriousness that once upon a time seekers of the truth used to drop strong acid in their eyes in order to see if they could maintain their equilibrium and composure in spite of the pain. The dysentery also vanished. I took my meals with Shri and shared the light fare that his servant Govinda Singh prepared for him with devotion. Again I performed my daily meditation in Shri's presence. The room seemed to be illuminated by an inner light, and when I opened my eyes I looked upon his countenance.

We had not decided whether to undertake the journey over the high mountain passes to Lake Manasarovar and Mt. Kailas in Tibet.

Shri asked me to come afterward to his home in Nasik and live there with him as his disciple, his son.

CHAPTER VII

PILGRIMAGE IN HIMALAYA

The pilgrims set out singing—A sacred locality—Statue of Hanuman, the monkey chief—Kaka-Bushunda, the world's Methuselah—State rest houses in the forest—Snake Mountain—A visit from a prince—Reports of floods and disaster—Shri decides to turn back—His teachings on the return journey

After morning meditation I sat and wrote a while. Then Shri Maharaj knocked on the door of the meditation room. "Now we must go!"

I put on my shoes as fast as possible. We went to the pilgrim shelter where I used to sleep.

Two embroidered quilts were spread out in an easy chair for Shri. This time I also sat on a chair in the midst of the ascetics, who squatted on the floor, and I could observe them unhindered.

The newly painted signs on their foreheads shone more brightly than ever. One man had smeared the entire upper part of his face with white earth. Behind him a young man crouched, scarcely more than a boy. The lines on his forehead were arched over the bridge of his nose so that they seemed to form a lotus flower. One man was as dark as a Negro. Two or three had magnificent white goatees. The old, well-preserved sannyasi who slept in the alley outside my room (and who paints his face as carefully as a woman) was there also, proud as a king.

We sang, led by a fat, good-natured monk who supervised the kitchen. He had taken special care of me, and this morning he had pressed me affectionately to his ample breast. Now it was he who gave the tone and started singing.

Suddenly his powerful voice changed and became quite shrill. Perspiration ran down his face and his eyes were filled with tears.

The departure took place with great ceremony. We marched in four columns. The prince, who had come a long way to take part in the festive occasion, led the parade with Shri Maharaj and me. Each of us waved a yellow flower in one hand. As we passed, people stood still in front of their houses and greeted us with folded hands. We marched over the flagstones of Almora's bazaar, along an endless street lined with shops on the ridge of the mountain. Sometimes we caught glimpses of the sharply sloping terraces on each side of the city.

This day, on which the first of the pilgrims set out on the road to Kailas—the earthly mountain home of Shiva—was a Monday, Shiva's day. The name hovering on our lips, the name of a god, bore us like a swinging, billowy sea.

The landscape spread out severely at our feet. Wisps of fog, many miles in length, coiled over it like the thick, whitish-gray snakes that encircle Shiva's throat.

As Shri had wished, we gathered in a small group separated from the other pilgrim throngs. It was an enchanted wandering, a world of richly undulating forest, with clear streams that reflected the sky. White streams of water flowed out of the bogs, the precipices, and even from trees that stood sky high. Rare and beautiful bright flowers rose softly out of the mire. The clear water in torrents and waterfalls seemed otherworldly. Heavenly water, the water of life! The place where the valley widens into a strip of forest meadow is called Jageshvar, after Shiva, "lord of the world."

This place, also called "little Kailas," is one of the most sacred places in the world. The great Kailas lies farther to the north, in Tibet, on the other side of the mighty, snow-covered crests of the Himalayas.

Jageshvar is a world-famous resort of pilgrims, but I did not come across a single dry-goods shop. There were a dozen or two humble wooden houses, but a world of wonderful, affectionately carved wood. The tree of life, the flowering wheel of the sun, and similar portrayals in red and blue, darkening with age, framed the windows and doors of the huts. On the shore of a lake lay the courtyard of the temple, surrounded by a wall. Inside were two large temples to Shiva, surrounded by numerous smaller ones. Balustrades with wooden roofs stretched on all sides from the slanting towers. The temple was not dedicated to Shiva the destroyer, but to Shiva "the conqueror of death."

I walked beside Shri in my long, orange-colored garment, across the courtyards and through the chilly, damp halls. At every door I received flowers. Finally, I stood before a red stone statue of Hanuman, chief of monkeys. His cheekbones were wide and high. He stood with his foot on a crushed monster, just as in Christian countries the archangel Michael tramps underfoot the plunging dragon. It is not with human strength that Hanuman conquered the monster, however. He stood deep in meditation, his hand on his forehead, aglow with spiritual strength.

Under a giant tree I saw another stone portrait of Hanuman, painted bright red as always. Hanuman held a mountain on his palm. As the story goes, when Rama's brother Lakshman had been wounded in battle, Rama ordered Hanuman to fetch a certain medicinal herb from the Himalayas. Hanuman flew in one second from the southernmost tip of India to the Himalayas, but he could not find the herb. Undaunted, he uprooted the whole mountain—with its forests and trees and herbs—and brought it to Rama. In this way, he thought, the desired herb would surely be there.

Shiva, Rama, and Hanuman all belong to this mountain and this forest. On temple walls, on tree trunks and precipice walls, the hermits who live in the rocky caves have written God's name in large letters: Rama, Rama, Rama. This name means "giver of joy." In his heart, Hanuman bears the name Rama, inscribed in letters of light. It is said that this divine name gives him his power.

There are about seven hundred thousand villages in India, and outside most of them is a small Hanuman temple. People say that Hanuman prevents the demons from entering the village.

I felt so content. We wandered and rode peacefully, rain or shine, through the endless forests, a wandering such as the artist Schwind or the poet Eichendorff depicted—and yet a holy wandering. One can leave the little village and trace the rushing river to its source, and from the gushing water it seems God himself leans down.

Thus the road led slowly up towards Kailas. Innumerable spiritual and physical events have taken place along this divine road, its slopes and its deep ravines. It is said that the oldest person in the world, Kaka-Bushunda, lives here, lost in deep meditation. He is many, many thousands of years old. He has seen the world go under and be reborn time and time again.

I sat on the mud floor under low rafters black with age, in a wing of one of the Shiva temples, a pilgrim shelter in which we had lodgings. A glaring kerosene lantern hung from one of the beams. One must be careful not to bump one's head on the ceiling. And yet this attic room was holy. Shri sat on an embroidered silk rug, as if on a throne. Opposite him, squatting on the floor, were men from ancient Brahman families who came to pay homage and discuss religious matters. Many also sought cures for their ailments. A few have come to submit a law case to Shri.

In the midst of throngs of people coming and going, and through the noise of singing pilgrims and the night roar of the river, I sat cross-legged, completely undisturbed. I just kept on writing.

We spent the last few nights in state-owned rest houses surrounded by endless stretches of forest-clad mountains. We have reached the highest point of the journey so far, a hut called Berinag, which means "king of the snakes." It was a very arduous march. The road went up and down, sometimes stretching through an endless deep valley, which was as hot as the tropics. Buffaloes, goats, agave, and bananas were everywhere. The road led straight upward in the glare of noon. The mountain chain of the Himalayas lay before us, behind three belts of forests, towering above them, inconceivably mighty. In the middle of it was a pyramid of ice about twenty-five thousand feet high—even higher than the mountains which reach the clouds. It is called Nanda Devi. Mountain upon mountain: Shiva's wife, Shiva's servant girls, Shiva's followers, all glittering with their icy rims in the sunlight. The nearest and therefore apparently highest was Shiva's trident, Mt. Trishul.

What is happening in Europe? Has war broken out?

After a hot bath and a satisfying meal, I felt refreshed. We were to spend two days on Snake Mountain. Around us are walnut trees, cedars, and others, unknown to me, bearing red flowers. We had to go into the valleys and up again to the mountain ridges four more times. We were only three days from Askot.

When I came riding alone through the pathless woods toward Berinag on Snake Mountain, I heard the singing of ancient Veda hymns nearby. It was a choir of schoolboys singing in Shri's honor the old songs which for thousands of years have been sung for kings and wise men. The boys carried a Gandhi banner that they had made themselves. When we returned some days later, the singing boys followed us again.

The mountain species of the Himalayas remind me of those in the Grand Canyon of North America. On picking up a stone, it almost frightens one to see it immediately crushed to dust. It was impossible to hammer a nail in one's shoe with the aid of a stone, and the soles of our shoes showed sad gaps. In Askot there would be a shoemaker, I was promised.

The Raja, the petty prince of Askot, visited us in our shelter, but he arrived with bad news. The peacefully winding River Kali, which we could see from our hut, had become wild and tempestuous in its upper course due to heavier rains than usual. All the bridges had been swept away, and the narrow road had collapsed in several places or had plunged into the abysses. The pilgrim throngs that had gone ahead of us had met with indescribable hardships. A few men had even died.

After a long silence, Shri decided to turn back. I had often been surprised that the friendly old man had been so aloof and indifferent toward Nityanand. Now I understood Shri's attitude. Nityanand's magnificent prophecies had not been realized. He who had solemnly declared that no one should die on this pilgrimage had made a mistake, and he had deceived himself and others. Shri received more distressing news. The merchants who had delivered kerosene lamps, umbrellas, raincoats, and other supplies for the pilgrimages had not been paid, and they held Nityanand responsible. He became involved in unpleasant lawsuits. People began to declare that he was an adventurer, that he had never been legally elected as Shankaracharya's successor, since he lacked the required knowledge of Sanskrit. It was out of place, however, for me to judge him. A newcomer to India may find it difficult to avoid being taken in, and it is not so easy to find an ascetic who really has dedicated his heart to God, as so many claim. The friends of God like to appear in disguise, and one needs His grace to recognize them.

I looked longingly from the heights of Askot upon the virgin green forests, the fields and the cloud-enveloped mountains in Nepal, which seemed to lay just below my feet, on the other side of the glittering stream Kali. It was a wonderful, smiling landscape. It was very disappointing for me not to be able to wander farther towards the north. Since I was in Shri's company, Tibet, the forbidden land, would not have been closed to me as to most Europeans. Shri had received an invitation from the viceroy of western Tibet. It was rumored that for several weeks, twenty-five horses had stood ready for us at the boundary.

"Wait until your time comes. Then Shiva will call you," said Shri.

For the next two days, the Raja's younger brother stayed with us in our bungalow. Though the members of his family once ruled the mighty kingdom of Kumaon—which stretched from Sikkim to Kabul—they now live like country squires or landed proprietors in the village of Askot. Like Rana, they too are descendants of the sun dynasty. Until a hundred years ago, all of the royal family bore the extra title "deva," god. When the English took their capital city,

Almora, in 1815, and they had to retire to Askot, they discarded that name.

I glanced once more at the winding, sun-drenched Kali river and then ran ahead of the others into the woods. This wandering back to Almora was full of strange joy. Four times again up the mountains and down into the tropically warm valleys, and then up the plateaus again, climbing steep paths. "It is not so important to go to the physical Kailas. The real Mt. Kailas, which lies in one's soul, that is what one must try to attain." Shri had written this to me long ago, at the beginning of our friendship.

Though I had apparently turned my back on Shiva's holy mountain, I felt nearer and nearer to it. I dreamt of him at night, and his icy head and glittering slopes were in my soul. On my way home, I once more traversed Himalaya.

In every shelter where we spent the night on our journey home, Shri imparted his teachings to me. He began in the shelter Tal, which lay in a murmuring forest ravine, the lowest point of the journey. The light from Himalaya's snow-capped mountains fell into the ravine.

"Today is the anniversary of that day when Krishna came down to earth," Shri said. "We shall celebrate it by reading together from the *Bhagavad-gita*. Vamandas, have you brought the Gita with you?"

"No, I have not brought it with me." The book had remained in Almora.

"What book have you, then?"

"Only *Vivekachudamani: The Crest Jewel of Discrimination*, by Shankaracharya."

Thus it happened that on one of the days when God had allowed himself to be born on Earth, I sat at the bottom of a deep ravine and read this magnificent book by Shankaracharya, which is atheistic in the end, declaring the world and the personal God to be illusions: No world exists, no God exists, only the all-consciousness, the Brahman without form.

As the journey progressed, I meditated on one phrase from the Upanishads which Shankaracharya had made the foundation of his conception: "Aham brahmasmi"—"I am Brahman." This powerful concept dwarfed even mountains, but secretly I was ashamed. I longed for the volume of the *Bhagavad-gita* which had been left behind in a trunk in Shri's little white house near Almora. I did not long for any particular verse; I longed for the book itself, the words Krishna had spoken to his disciple and friend Arjuna.

When I returned to Almora and the outcast street-sweepers raised clouds of rank white dust with their big brooms, I thought rejoicingly, "That, too, belongs to him! It is Krishna's dust they are raising!"

CHAPTER VIII

ANANDAPITH
THE HOME OF BLESSEDNESS

Vrindavan, birthplace of Krishna—Flowers and beggars—Shri's house in Nasik—Building a temple to Dattatreya—The Casteless—Krishna Chaitanya

It was my birthday on the day of my return to Almora, and it seemed as if I had never been away. The dried-up, terraced land-scape had become greener. The grain grew tall. The rivers were swelling, but the water was clear. And trees that were strange to me flowered like tall candelabra with white flames. The essence of each day was meditation.

And thus we finally left Almora, and traveled to Nasik.

We passed over many wide rivers, green copses and temples on either side. In ancient houses people sang hymns to the gods by the light of candles or oil lamps. The narrow-gauge railway leading into Himalaya had its starting point in Mathura, and there our journey was interrupted a few hours.

It was early morning. I drove with Shri to the city where, according to tradition, Krishna was born five thousand years ago. A wild, noisy Asiatic crowd packed the cobbled streets, strained by great four-wheeled buffalo carts and cows leisurely stretched on the ground. Beggars ravaged by leprosy and merchants struck clam-orously onto our car. Through a stunted hot copse that had once been a flowering virgin forest, we drove to Vrindavan, where

50

Krishna had spent his happy youth among the shepherds. We planned to spend a few months there during the cooler season the following year.

I sat in the shade with Shri for a while on one of the steps leading down to the stream called Yamuna. We took off our shoes and socks, and stretched our legs into the shimmering water.

After the long trek in Himalaya, one of my toes had swelled feverishly, throbbing and bluish-red, probably full of puss. "Perhaps Yamuna's holy water will heal my foot," I remarked, half jesting.

"It will certainly be healed," Shri answered in all seriousness.

It was wonderful to feel the soft, warm water on my face, hands and tired feet. Wise-eyed fishes swam confidently up to us and away again. When I looked closer, I saw that what I had taken for fishes were really the heads and necks of large tortoises.

Shri had bought flowers and garlands in order to have small change for the innumerable beggars. At his suggestion, I sacrificed the flowers in the river, took up the clear water by cupping my hands, and let it slowly run out again. A priest on the shore recited a prayer. Afterward, the priest placed a mussel shell filled with red dye beside me on the wet stone step. I dipped my finger in the dye and painted the red sign on the head of one of the tortoises. Then the priest painted the holy sign of Krishna on our foreheads. I remembered the Hindu story of God's incarnation as a tortoise that lifted the world out of the ocean after a mighty flood.

When we reached Nasik the following day, my foot was completely healed.

For Indians, Nasik is one of the great pilgrimage sites. Members of the old families of India journey to Nasik to visit their family tree in the temple.

Shri's house Anandapith, "the home of blessedness," looked like a country manor. He received his guests in an enormous room where the cushions and the white clothes that were his seat were spread on a tiger skin. The adjacent room was his large meditation room. Pictures of gods and teachers, decorated with garlands, hung all over the walls. I was to meditate in his reception room with the door open at the threshold, so I could be near him and yet not disturb him.

At night the door between my bedroom and Shri's stood wide open. Whenever I awoke at three or three-thirty in the morning, the grand old man was sitting in the blue light of the stars, meditating for the troubled world.

In the afternoon, Shri took me on strolls through his property. He was a master builder. At the time, he was supervising the construction of a Dattatreya temple. The beautiful framework was ready, and the cupola shone like a white flower.

According to Hindu belief, Dattatreya is one of the saviours who has helped redeem the world. He is portrayed with three heads and six arms, since he is said to have combined the strength of Brahma, Vishnu, and Shiva when he taught wisdom and poise to humanity. In his six hands, Dattatreya holds the lotus flower and sounding mussel of the Creator, the judgment wheel and scepter of the Maintainer, and the trident and water jug of the Destroyer. Deep symbolism is hidden within the weapons borne by the three gods, who are actually one.

Shri always carried a little ivory statue of Dattatreya in a blue velvet bag. He set up this statue wherever he spent the night, and he placed flowers at its base. He sang songs for me that were written to Dattatreya. "He is my guru, my spiritual teacher," he said.

The inside of the new temple was still empty. The word AUM shone in letters of gold above the entrance. The marble sculpture of the three-headed Dattatreya was not yet ready.

When I drove to town I dressed in European clothes, but in Shri's home and on his property I wore a *dhoti*, a garment of thin white cloth that the wind could blow through. It was delightful in the heat.

The bananas were slowly ripening, and it was the first time the young plants in Shri's garden were bearing. They spread out like hands with many green fingers. Sometimes they stretched upward like candles in a candelabrum. But the most delicious fruit of all was the mango. There is a sweetness and aroma in mangoes that is not found in any other fruit, but unfortunately they cannot stand shipping.

I accompanied Shri on a visit to a mango grove owned by one of his friends. Shri often stayed with this friend when he wandered about as a hermit, as he had done so for many years. The fruit hung by the hundreds on long, thin green stems from the crown of an old, giant tree. They were golden-yellow, purple-red, dozens of different species, with different shades of color. "Like parrots," said Shri. The fruit looked like the gilded and silvered nuts on a Christmas tree. Between the mango groves were long stretches of grape vines. The grapes of Nasik were very famous, though I had not tasted them yet—the harvest would not be ripe until April. Instead of lattices as supports, thin trees with high narrow tops had been planted. One walked beneath the grape vines as if they were an arch of leaves. Here and there were wheat fields, wells, and teams of buffalo pulling up the biblical leather sack, dripping with water, from deep, round well-curbs.

We took the main road from Agra to Bombay through an endless alley of Indian fig trees, many of which were six hundred years old. Here and there were unbelievably miserable mud huts with roofs of rusty sheet metal, homes to some of the millions of Indians who live on the verge of starvation.

Even today casteless men and women go about with brooms on their shoulders, cleaning the latrines. Many believe that God has commanded and pre-ordained this. If one of the "untouchables" thirsts for knowledge—this seldom happens—then he is in most cases so brave and such a lover of truth that he can be recognized as a Brahman. The great teachers of wisdom, the rishis of ancient India, had the right to make a shudra (a member of the lowest caste) or a casteless person a Brahman.

"But if one breaks the law of caste blindly," says the Gita, "confusion enters, and all order disappears. Then God himself must descend upon earth in order to save humanity."

Shri was clapping his hands. This meant that he was calling me, silently telling me to begin my meditation. There was a guest in his room, and they were conversing, sometimes loudly, sometimes softly. Shri wore a wreath of flowers on his breast and held flowers in his hand.

I sat down for meditation and chased away the thought that kept disturbing me: "Why did he call me now? Why does he wish me to meditate in the presence of a stranger?"

I had once asked Shri, "If my eyes and ears disturb me during meditation, what shall I do?"

His answer was: "Say to them kindly: Eye, your task just now is not to see outwardly, but inwardly, to see the spiritual light. Ear, your task is not to listen to outward things, but to the music within."

It helped me concentrate. When I arose, the guest had left, and Shri too had concluded his meditation. My glance fell on a picture on the wall that I had not noticed before, a young man of golden luster, standing on the shore of a river. Shri told me that it was Krishna Chaitanya, who lived in Bengal around the time America was discovered. He was considered by many to be a reincarnation of Krishna. Bengal still resounds with songs in praise of him.

CHAPTER IX

THE MAJESTY OF GOD

The tale of Krishna and Narada, the great wise man—Mighty mantra about Rama—Reading the Bible with Shri

Shri's meditation room in Nasik often seemed coated with gold from the spiritual strength that had accumulated there over the years. In this room and in the large, airy workroom next to it, I listened to many a story related by my teacher.

The first of the legends which I shall repeat here originates from Krishna Chaitanya himself. Apparently, he describes the divine majesty that rules our universe, illustrating it with flowering fantasy. But this is only metaphor.

Our universe is corruptible. The power of a Brahma, ruler of the universe, is also corruptible, according to Indian belief, even if it lasts a billion years. The inner sight of the disciple, therefore, is indirectly steered toward God's incorruptible kingdom, which in not of this world.

Chaitanya once related the following to his disciples.

KRISHNA AND BRAHMA

Krishna's many-sided divinity surpasses all that can be expressed in words. Therefore, I shall tell of only a fraction of his divinity, that which is revealed in the majesty of the universe.

One day Brahma went to the castle of the Almighty to visit the Lord. The gatekeeper bore the news to Krishna, who asked, "Which Brahma is it?" The gatekeeper returned and repeated the question: "Krishna wishes to know which Brahma you are."

Impatient and dumbfounded, the creator answered, "Tell him that I am the four-headed Brahma."

When the gatekeeper had received permission from Krishna, he allowed the creator to enter. Brahma bowed at Krishna's feet, and the latter asked him the reason for his visit. Brahma answered, "My Lord, first answer one question. What did you mean when you asked, 'Which Brahma?'"

Krishna smiled and fell into meditation. There immediately appeared countless Brahmas—with ten heads, with twenty, with a hundred, with a thousand, a million, yes, with a billion heads; it was beyond anyone's power to count. Shivas came with millions upon millions of heads. Indras revealed themselves with millions of eyes. Seeing all this, the four-headed Brahma almost lost command over himself, like a rabbit encircled by a troop of elephants. The Brahmas bowed before the throne of Krishna, touching it with their crowns. Tones streamed from the throne as if the crowns were singing hymns of praise to the throne of Krishna. With folded hands, the Brahmas, Shivas, and other divinities glorified Krishna thus. "Lord, great is your mercy toward us, for you allow us to behold your feet. O infinite happiness, you have called upon us and received us in your service. If you command, we shall bear you upon our heads."

Krishna said, "I longed to see you, and therefore I called upon you to come here. Are you satisfied? Have you anything to fear from the demons?"

They answered, "Thanks to your grace, we are victorious everywhere. And finally you have appeared upon earth and destroyed the burden of sin that was dragging it down into the abyss."

Then Krishna dismissed all the Brahmas, and they returned to their homes, bowing deeply in farewell.

The four-headed Brahma of our universe threw himself at the feet of Krishna and said, "Today I have been reminded anew of something that I once knew very well."

Krishna replied, "Although your universe is five hundred million miles in circumference, it is yet very small. Therefore, you have only four heads. Other universes measure a thousand million, a hundred thousand million, and millions of millions of miles in their circumference, and their Brahmas have a number of heads in proportion thereto. And I bear all the kingdoms in the spaces of the world. My divinity is immeasurable. Who will try to perceive the breadth of my occult divinity?"

From the infinity of God, leading back to warmer regions nearer earth, is another story. This one is almost a cosmic joke, yet one can feel the pulse of eternity in it.

BRAHMA, VISHNU, AND SHIVA

Shiva once had a seed of a thought: "What would happen if I stopped destroying?" This thought had hardly entered his head when Brahma said, "Listen, what would happen if I stopped creating?" Just then Vishnu appeared and said, "What do you think would happen if I stopped maintaining the universe?" "I shall stop destroying!" "I shall stop creating!" "I shall stop preserving!" the gods exclaimed and clapped their hands, amused.

A wagon came rolling out of the unknown. Amazed, the gods saw that the wagon contained nothing but eggs. When an egg fell upon the ground, its shell burst and a new Brahma stepped out. When another egg burst, a Vishnu emerged, and from a third egg came a new Shiva. And new eggs kept falling out of the wagon.

Then the gods became frightened, and clasped their hands and threw themselves before the Almighty. Suddenly, the wagon disappeared and Brahma, Vishnu, and Shiva resumed their work.

We are taken still deeper into Maya's great river of delusion in the story of the great wise man Narada. This powerful rishi is considered Krishna's eye, for he wanders the three worlds looking for beings worthy of liberation. But when God desires, even

Narada can fall under the powerful spell of delusion, as this tale illustrates.

KRISHNA AND NARADA

Once upon a time Narada visited Krishna. The latter stood outside His palace and invited his guest to dine with him, whereupon Narada thanked him and went to bathe in a nearby river, telling Krishna he would be back in five minutes.

The rishi dived into the river, but to his surprise he was immediately changed into a woman. Amazed, he touched his long hair, his breasts and his body. He still remembered that he was Narada, the great wise man, but the longer he remained in the water, the fainter this memory grew. He became Naradi, the young woman. When a young man walked along the bank of the river, she took his hand and he led her to his home, where she bore him innumerable children. Gradually, her beauty vanished. The children cried and clamored. All the troubles of life enveloped her. She became ill and old, and in this condition she cried to God. At that moment she became Narada again, and the Lord stood at the entrance of his palace. "Narada, the five minutes have passed. Our meal is ready!"

Narada had dived into the waters of Maya, of which Krishna is master.

This tale is very popular in India. A moving picture has even been made of the story, and it has run a long time at a great many cinemas throughout the country. The most successful films in India, strangely enough, are not the parlor comedies, gangster films, or adventure and criminal stories, where sex appeal plays the chief role, as in the West. The films shown to full houses in India are portrayals of the Almighty God, and of the messengers he sends to earth.

I once sat in the middle of an audience in one of the cheapest seats, a rough wooden bench in an overflowing theater that resembled a big barn. I was probably the only white man in the crowd of spectators. Rats chased one another at our feet. This bothered no one, however, because we were completely fascinated by the performance.

Suddenly, an enraptured cry sounded through the hall. My neighbors on each side of me, strangers, gripped my arms intensely in their excitement. They asked me breathlessly if I, a European, could really see, really understand that God had intervened.

I nodded assent.

On the white sheet before us, a miraculously liberated wise man tumbled out of his dark prison onto a street that streamed with light. He spread his arms and jubilantly sang one of God's names: "Rama!" The crowds of people around him joined in his singing rejoicingly: "Rama! Rama!" Not only the people on the white sheet, but nearly all of the spectators in the theater had begun to sing so loudly that I thought the roof would cave in: "Rama! Rama! Rama!" With all the power in their lungs they sang the mighty mantra about Rama, who lifts and cleanses the fallen.

The spectators then quieted down and were listening. The hero, who had patiently endured so much suffering, was softly praying to God. It was the same thousand-year-old prayer that Shri had often repeated for me.

"Thou art our father. Thou art our mother. Thou art our beloved friend. Thou art the source of our strength. Thou who bearest the burden of the universe, help us bear the little burden of this our life."

One must not imagine that Indian religious films are insipidly sweet or that they have the skin-deep beauty of an oleograph. Perhaps they are a little too long and drawn out for Western taste, but they are full of humor and of harsh or apt illustrations from the life of the people, and some scenes really are masterpieces. At a worldwide film competition held in Venice, one of these Indian religious films received the highest honors ever granted a film.

I lost myself in the Orient for several months, but gradually the East and the West began to strive for some kind of alliance within me. When I read from the *Bhagavad-gita* with Shri in the evenings, the portals of Germanic antiquity, the runes, suddenly opened up before me. I translated from the Eddas, from Voluspa, for Shri.

For a while, I also read from the Bible daily for Shri. I read about Abraham, Joseph, Solomon, Zedekias, Elias, Josias, and above all from Paul's "Letters from Rome" and "Letters from Corinth." Shri thought that one of the darkest shadows of the Old Testament were the words, "Of dust thou art, to dust thou returnest." "No!" he said. "Of light thou art, and to light thou return!"

CHAPTER X

INDIAN FEAST

Shri's birthday celebrations—The village postmaster—Watching the monkeys—Divali, the Festival of Light—Paying evening calls—Gaiety and good feeling

At the time of the full moon in March, Shri celebrated his fifty-ninth birthday. All of us were invited to celebrate at Rana's home in Sadras. Rana and a Brahman, a stranger to me, performed a long ritual. Shri's disciples, his grown-up sons and daughters, and invited guests took part in this ceremony. I understood only a few words of the old Sanskrit Vedic hymns that they sang, in alternating chorus, as they sat at Shri's feet. "Shanti, shanti, shanti! Peace, peace, peace!"

Shri was deluged with flowers. When the singing was over, milk and water were poured over him. Each of us took a drop of the fluid that had been poured over his body, and we stretched our hand over the lighted candles placed before him. When I bowed at his feet and touched them with my forehead, full of the deepest affection and gratitude, he embraced me fondly, laid his hands on my cheeks and said, "I am glad you are here today, Vamandasji."

The syllable *ji* is a friendly form, which Shri seldom used. It is really the ancient word *arya*—noble. I felt as if I had fallen upon a bed of roses.

Towards evening, another service was held for the numerous guests. Some petty princes from the neighborhood also attended. In the middle of the vacated dining-room on the bottom floor, four banana plants had been placed in square formation, symbolizing

61

the creation of the world. In front of them were flowers, fruits, sweets, rows of lighted candles and glowing incense sticks. All this was a sacrifice to the Highest in gratitude for His creation, and had been borne there with upraised hands. Later, it was distributed among the guests.

One of the guests, a disciple of Shri's, was an elderly man, postmaster in a little south Indian village. Many years ago, while on one of his wanderings, Shri had entered his post office in search of some information. The postmaster had been moved so deeply by Shri's appearance and saintliness that he looked him up the very same day. A feeling of humble affection and respect had been the result of this meeting with Shri, and henceforth, when the postmaster had a couple of free days, he would ask Shri if he might visit him. On this day, he had come to greet him on his birthday. In two years, he was to be pensioned, and at that time he planned to remain with Shri and serve him. He said to me, "How happy you must be, who have Shri's blessing, and can be with him constantly!"

Rana was like a brother to me. He lived in a fine, cheerful house, something between a bungalow and a palace, built upon smooth white pillars. Great trees surrounded it, and the walls were painted a clear green color. Two skins hung on the walls, those of a tiger and a tigress that Rana had shot. The ceilings were paneled in white or brown. In front of the house was a green lawn with many-hued, bright flowers on long stalks; trees laden with fruit; and old, knotty deciduous trees. A dozen Indian servants were kept busy seeing that the plot of grass remained fresh and green by watering it with pails of water. All the country in that area was yellow and dry, burned up by the glowing sun. All the roads were covered with a fine dust, which lay there like soft, down pillows—until barefoot beggars and wandering hordes of animals raised great clouds of it. In their midst flew giant, shrieking peacocks; camels and hordes of buffalo wandered over the yellow steppes. The leafy treetops were alive with white squirrels and great, silver-gray monkeys. One of Rana's many servants had a full-time job keeping these monkeys somewhat at bay.

He shot at them with a bow and a rubber-tipped arrow to frighten the most impudent ones. The monkeys hopped onto the car tires when Rana fetched us, and they danced at night on the roof of the tent in which I slept when the house was filled with guests. This tent was exceedingly pleasant. Like those used by Indian officers, it was made of double canvas as a protection against the sun. It contained a carpet, a bed, a lounge chair, an armchair and a desk. A sort of verandah and a bathroom were also included.

It was good to lie in the lounge chair and look up at the newly sprouted leafage and watch the monkeys.

Shri approved of the fact that the apes played on the roof of my tent at night. "They protect you. Hanuman, the chief of the monkeys, is protecting you," he said jokingly.

My guru's birthday was on a Sunday, at full moon. The Indians do not calculate their birthdays according to a certain date. They say that they were born at full moon, or with the new moon in a certain month, or so many days with the waxing or waning moon. The gleaming white moon rules the year.

On the second day of the feasting, Monday, Shiva's day, Rana invited all the Brahmans of the district, about two hundred, to dinner in Shri's honor. They ate outdoors on the ground. Several cooks had been hired for the day, for Rana had some thirty other guests at the same time, who dined in the hall on the first floor.

For several days the shaded part of the courtyard had been watered to settle the dust and make the ground hard and even. Now the Brahmans sat there with their legs crossed, in two long rows facing one another, waiting. There were old men and small boys among them, and all the men were naked from the waist up, except for the Brahman cord about their throats. The lower part of their bodies was swathed in gaily colored blue, red, green, or purple garments. The women sat apart, also in long rows, gaily dressed. Some of them sat in small groups of their own, divided according to caste. Patient, silent, and peaceful, they sat and waited nearly an hour, for it took a long time to prepare food for so many. A European crowd would have become noisy and restless.

The waiters gradually came and placed a big plate, made of banana leaves plaited together, on the ground before each guest. After that came bowls, plaited likewise, for the rich soup called dahl. Large brown balls of sugar, flour, and melted butter were placed on the dishes. Those who wished to have two or three such balls were given them, and those who were satisfied with one implied so with a quiet gesture of the hand. The servants waiting on them, going the length of the long rows, dug deep into the metal pots with their hands, serving piles of rice on the banana-leaf dishes, and they poured melted butter over the rice. Small piles of vegetables were placed around the rice. Various kinds of bread, thin as leaves, were served. All this time, the guests waited quietly until the host gave a sign. Then in chorus they sang a hymn to Shiva, and after that the feasting began. The servants tirelessly brought in new dishes, more rice, thin bread, and sugar balls. The apes in the trees looked on greedily.

It is a fine art to eat elegantly and neatly with one's hands. In spite of many efforts, I am still far from mastering it. First the rice must be carefully kneaded with the right hand, then soaked with the water from the vegetables and put into one's mouth. Bread must be broken with the right hand only, with no assistance from the left. These guests, most of them simple people, had mastered the art.

The new moon in October, called Divali, is considered the luckiest day of the year. On that day, Rama killed the ten-headed demon Ravan. In India, it is the first day of school, and armies used to set out for battle on that lucky day.

Divali means festival of light. It is also a thanksgiving feast for the harvest, the first day of winter, and the first day of the calendar year.

This feast uplifts one like a wave on the sea.

The fireworks begin as early as dawn. From above, from below, and from all sides, four- or five-year-old boys were setting off firecrackers. They popped under our feet, and sparks flew from left to right when we walked through the streets. The whole land celebrated and feasted four days in succession.

At five o'clock in the morning, before sunrise, people bathed and began to eat. Between meals one munched pastry made of achanti nuts, and cakes filled with coconut pulp. For dinner, sweet saffron-yellow rice and other dishes that were new to me were served.

Shri Maharaj's family, including his sons, daughters, sons- and daughters-in-law, grandchildren, other guests, and their servants, all sat on very low seats with their legs crossed under them. We sat in very exact order. Our host had a low table and a seat with a back to it. I, too, had a seat with a back, but like all the other guests who had no support, my table consisted of a giant green banana leaf spread on the floor. Around every "table" an ornament resembling a lotus flower was painted in purple-red chalk on the slabs of the floor. Silver bowls and dishes were refilled constantly with vegetables. The food was placed in little heaps directly on the banana leaves. The meal began with rice, dahl, different vegetables, salads, and butter, followed by sweets. And finally rice, vegetables, and yogurt milk.

The table was lower than the seats. It was difficult to reach down to it. My feet were numb from crossing my legs under me. When the meal was over, I limped painfully out of the room, to the amusement of the others, who laughed aloud.

I joined in their laughter and was glad that they laughed at my behavior and table manners, which were not yet genuinely Indian.

In the evening we set out to pay calls. We went from one shop to another through the town, which was brightly lit and filled with rejoicing people. There were no customers. People were out in order to wish one another happiness. Everywhere we were received joyfully. A pleasant-smelling fluid was spread out on the right hand and sprayed on our heads. "The harvest was good," exclaimed the proprietor with satisfaction. A dish containing spices was offered to us, and we were given betel leaves to chew and bunches of flowers. Wreaths were placed around our necks, and we returned home with flowers and pastries, every pocket bulging.

Nowhere did we see any beer served, nor wine, nor any other intoxicating drink. I did not see anyone drunk. Not only Hindus, but many Mohammedans as well celebrated this festival of light. Outside the poorest mud huts, the lights burned on this evening, huts that housed people so poor that they could not afford to light candles more than once a year.

We were invited to dinner by Thakore Sahib, the ruler of the state of Vasana. Thakore Sahib, one of the petty princes of India, was a young widower. His private income plus that of the state he ruled did not exceed 40,000 rupees, but he had a Chevrolet car and a prime minister with a monthly salary of a hundred rupees.

For this occasion I dressed in formal European attire, including a dinner jacket and a pair of white shoes I had never used. I sat in my shirt sleeves like everyone else, on a seat hardly as high as the length of a finger, and "took to my fingers" from a great oval metal plate. Before me lay sweet and sour dishes, many unknown to me by name, arranged around a central heap of rice. Everyone mixed the yellow lemon pudding, the beans, buttermilk, yogurt and the many kinds of bread according to individual preference. Everything tasted marvelous.

The prince's palace reminded me of Odysseus' royal dwelling on Ithaka, as one might imagine it. The herdsmen, who looked after cows, came and went. The castle was built in three stories with steep wooden steps and beamed ceilings. It was originally an old manor house, magnificent but dilapidated, all wonderfully carved gray wood. Every support that held up a rafter or a ceiling was decorated with carving; for example, a rider with shield and sword and wig-ornamented helmet, with mythical animals on both sides. Windows and doors stood wide open. In spite of the heat of noon, a cool breeze refreshed the entire house. Rocking chairs or wide sofas swung on heavy copper chains in all the rooms. Each link of the chain was made of small pictures of the gods.

Here, too, was one servant whose only duty was to chase away the monkeys that wanted to climb up on the roof.

INDIAN FEAST

From the dwelling of the prince on the top of the hill, we drove downward in curves and turns, on frightful roads that were full of holes, deep ruts, and thick dust. Around the country castle a group of ramshackle mud huts clung to the mountain slope.

CHAPTER XI

SHIVA'S DRUM

Harvest on the Indian plains—Alan, the young American chemist—
The rishi Vasistha, guru of kings—Maya, the handmaid of God—
Drums in the temple of Shiva—Mountain of the goddess
Arbuda—News of German invasion of Czechoslovakia—Kaliyuga,
Age of Darkness—The avatar of Kaliyuga.

The sun shone hot on the Indian plains. The crops were harvested, and the stubble fields lay there staring, yellow, burned, like a desert. Worn out after a long illness, I sat day after day beside the window in a house near Kolhapur and watched the two-wheeled harvest wagons, drawn by buffaloes, waddle along the road. The dust raised by the clumsy wheels filled the air and penetrated one's lungs. When the road became blocked somewhere, one could see endless rows of heavily loaded wagons standing still, as far away as the distant wavy line that the hills formed on the horizon. In the evenings and at early dawn, long before sunrise, I heard the buffalo drivers' spurring call and their incessant singing. The thousands of wagon loads of golden hay they were driving did not belong to them. It all belonged to the Maharaja of Kolhapur.

Half-naked men stamped to the accompaniment of singing on the yellow wall of grass that grew taller and taller, a security against future starvation. This reserve was all the more necessary since this state did not import meat and prohibited cow slaughter.

I suddenly escaped the glowing plains and found myself on a high plateau. The sun was no longer a bitter, hostile star, the countenance of the god of death, who burned up the earth.

68

Sunlight flooded through the the chilly wind, which blew through the mountain tops. In the evenings, a young American chemist named Alan sat shivering with Shri Maharaj and I on the cold stone slabs outside our bungalow. A cold night wind shook the windows and jerked open the doors of the house. It was wonderful to freeze a little. But the first letter that Shri dictated to me was an urgent request for warm blankets.

Alan was a thirty-one-year-old chemist. He had met Shri when the latter was traveling in America nine years ago. He had taught himself Sanskrit and saved money to travel to India and become Shri's disciple. Alan had tried his hand at many different trades in order to reach his goal. He had fought bravely against depression and unemployment in America, even after losing a position with a leasing and hiring agent—dismissed for sitting in an empty room, gazing out of the window, and studying Sanskrit during working hours. He had also worked in an ammunition factory, in a whiskey distillery, and in similar places, "in Shiva the Destroyer's shop," remarked Shri. After a few months, his usual fate overtook him again. But on being given notice this time, he received the news joyfully, informing his employer that he had already intended to leave. "Leaving! Where are you going?" the man had asked. "To India." His employer had grasped him warmly by the hand. "Yes, that is right, go to India, for you belong there. And may I ask what you intend to do there?" "I shall study yoga," was the answer.

Alan had only a few hundred dollars, with which he was very careful. He had chosen the slowest and cheapest cargo boat he could find. The trip had lasted six weeks, in a third-class berth, with long detours via Scotland, Gibraltar, and Marseilles. He was a bit upset and confused after the long journey by sea, and by his first acquaintance with that part of the tropical world where we sat shivering in front of Shri, on the cold stone floor of the bungalow Shanti Nivas, the home of peace, high up on Mt. Abu.

Alan's daily grievance was that he could not sit according to Indian fashion, as I could, with his legs crossed under him on the floor. His knees were too stiff. In a bitter fight against this stiffness he had broken both knees in America, but this did not help the elasticity of the joints. Exasperated, he squatted on the floor and exercised daily to conquer this stiffness bit by bit. When he took off his glasses one could see his good, clean, shy, boyish face. He was mercilessly honest, above all with himself. He could get very angry when I used similes that he considered exaggerated or too poetic. But secretly he, too, was a poet, according to what he confessed to me long afterward. There had come a time in his life when he had painfully cut himself off from all poetry and hardened himself against it.

My little room had a window facing east. On Mt. Abu I succeeded often in getting up before sunrise. I would go out on the stone terrace and look over the crowns of the palm trees, towards the east where the sun was to rise. When I sang the mantra to the sun, facing the heavens as they became brighter, the pious intensity of countless humans streamed through me.

The first crystal ray gleamed through the feathery treetops. The disc of the sun rose. I sang:

Take away the golden disc
that I may see thy true form…

Soon Alan made his appearance, a bit sleepy, and we wandered over the mountain. It was during these wonderful morning hours that we made our first voyages of discovery on Mt. Abu. In the beginning we generally ran home to fetch our coats before setting out, for there was a raw morning wind.

Abu is enveloped in legends. In some of the old sagas about the gods, it is said that Abu is the son of Himalaya.

The mountain is pitted with caves and grottos where ascetics have meditated since time immemorial. On the wooded slopes of the mountain, where beasts of prey hide and frightened apes wander in the trees, two ancient rishis once had their huts. We spent one day in the hermit dwelling of the rishi called Vasistha, deep in a luxuriant wilderness at the edge of a precipice. The old sagas relate that

Vasistha was for thousands of years the guru of all the kings of the Sun dynasty, the same lineage to which my friend Rana belonged. With Rana, who had come on a visit, we read from a manuscript said to have been written by Vasistha. It is called Yoga Vasistha, or the Great Ramayana, and it contains teachings that were given to the avatar King Rama. This work expresses great sorrow over the transitoriness of the world.

Near one of the many heights is a row of underground caves that had been hewn into a temple in ancient times. There in the darkness is Arbuda, ruler of the transitory world. The whole mountain was originally called Arbuda, which is one of the many names for Maya. One must wander through many caves to enter into her holy shrine. On each side of the portal built of rocks, her sign, the trident, is painted in red and surrounded by the sun and the moon. Maya, ruler of the earth and servant of God, descended from heaven into the darkness of earth. Her countenance was black. I stood before her statue reverently, barefoot like the others.

Since then I have seen and entered many temples of Maya. This handmaid of God is worshiped in India under many names, portrayed in many forms and in many different colors. I once entered a Maya temple in another wild mountain region. This temple was also hewn out of a mountain cave, but the frightening, fiery red statue there rose above me in giant proportions.

I looked anxiously at the priests. They looked like dwarfs where they stood, high up on the dismal cliff shelves behind the statue, pouring cool water on Maya's glowing body, as if to appease her wrath. The terrible Goddess held ten spears in her outstretched hands. The ten spears indicated the points of the compass—north, south, east and west—the points lying between these—northwest, northeast, southeast and southwest—and the Zenith and Nadir. Maya's spear holds back those who try to forcibly enter God's realm for selfish purposes, without love, and with a desire that has not been chastened.

Every morning Alan and I wandered around Maya's mountain. Every afternoon and evening we strolled together with Shri between rounded hillocks of reddish stone, and through groves of flowering old mango trees, which had a stupefying perfume. We seldom met anyone, for although Mt. Abu is a famous health resort in India, there was only one guest in the spacious Hotel Rajputana. Only the buffaloes observed us. Monkeys hopped from one treetop to another. On the empty roads one could imagine the tread of the devout who have walked barefoot on their way to the cliff temple of Arbuda.

Sometimes we unexpectedly caught a glimpse of the plains to the south or the west below us, the great glittering yellow desert and its dried-up riverbeds.

Every morning and evening we heard reverberating sounds from a copper drum in the great temple of Shiva.

"What does that beating of drums mean?" we asked.

"When a soul, an Atman, awakes," Shri replied, "then Maya also awakes. She lies stiff, wrapped in dark night, not only in cosmos, but buried deep in the body of Man. Rejoicing, her liberated power rises from the depths of the human body, up through the heart and the head to Brahma's thousand-petaled lotus flower, to God. When the stream of Maya rushes through the lotus flower of the inner heart, the yogi hears a vibrating tone in his heart, which is not perceptible to the physical ear."

People who have not yet awakened must be reminded of this tone through the daily reverberation of Shiva's drum.

"Buddha, who is included among the great avatars of God by us Hindus, has probably known this experience," Shri continued. "After his meditation under the Bodhi tree, 'the tree of enlightenment,' Siddhartha awoke completely and left for Shiva's city, Benares, singing:

> The kingdom of truth I shall find.
> To the city of Benares I am bound.
> Loudly ringing in worlds of darkness,
> the drum of immortality shall sound.

Almost every day toward evening, we wandered with Shri to the great white temple of Shiva on the shore of a mountain lake. Its

pinnacled roof rose majestically above a courtyard and pilgrim shelter. It was here the copper drums sounded every evening. Alan once
shyly touched the drum with his finger, and it resounded with a deep
tone. We sat on the slope of a promontory and Shri instructed us.
Sometimes we were silent and observed the animals that played
about us undisturbed. Beetles and ants in the grass, lizards that dart-
ed away in a flash, and chameleons that glided quickly forward all
stopped suddenly as if frozen stiff, then disappeared again, often
changing color: first emerald green, then purple red. Swarms of ants
danced over the lake as rare birds flew overhead. Thoughtfully Shri
looked up at the ants and the colorful birds. "Nothing but atmas."

One day, as we walked down to the lake, we happened to see
notices with giant headlines in the entrance of Hotel Rajputana. We
read: "The Germans march into Czechoslovakia. Prague occupied."
The rumbling of Shiva's drums—and world history—had reached us.

Alan was very downcast that evening. While we sat on a cliff
promontory above the glittering surface of the water, he talked about
America. In his youth, during times of depression, many people in
that wealthy country had lived on the verge of suicide because they
feared unemployment and starvation. He told of mothers who regretted having given birth to their children.

"In our own times so many people suffer from fear—fear that
conditions might get worse, that they might get cancer, that Hitler
and his machinery should reach us. Do you believe, Shri, that Hitler
can reach us? Do you believe it is possible that a great new war can
break out that will convert the world to a heap of ruins?"

"In Kaliyuga, anything can happen," answered Shri seriously.

Alan jumped up and stomped his foot. "Kaliyuga! I abhor such
high-sounding names!" he exclaimed bitterly. "It doesn't matter
whether they are invented by rishis or by Goebbels. The *Dritte Reich*
and the irrevocable divine plan of the world...I cannot see any dif-
ference. They are fine phrases, all of them! Where does free will
come in? What becomes of the atma if one is hopelessly left in the

power of Hitler or of Kaliyuga? Perhaps you are going to assert now that the dictators of today are atmas? They are nothing but demons!"

"Demons are atmas also," said Shri emphatically. "We must fight the demons; God delivers them. The dictators you fear are dwarfs compared to the mighty demons that ruled the earth in the days of yore, when Krishna came. But when Krishna killed them or placed his foot upon their heads, they entered his divine light."

The young American stared sullenly at the ground. As plaintively as a sleepy boy, he remarked, "I don't want to live in Kaliyuga, the age of darkness. Why can't we have a golden age?"

"The golden age prevails always in the awakened soul," Shri said.

The skies and the water had paled. We walked home in the light of the rising moon and in the shadow of dark trees. A breeze heavy with the perfume of flowers swept past us now and again, and at times we were engulfed by the delicious fragrance of a mango grove in full bloom.

The three of us, Shri in the middle, stepped out of the shadow of the last group of trees into a moonlit meadow in front of our white summer house, Shanti Nivas, which rose in the midst of murmuring palms toward a sky full of stars.

"Is it not really a home of peace?" asked Shri gladly, and stroked Alan's ash-blond hair lightly, almost with a gesture of blessing.

We lingered awhile in the moonlight on the grass of the meadow. Alan's gaze was fixed on the ground. "Shri," he began after a while with a voice that was still troubled. "Shri, during all this period of Kaliyuga, since the time of Christ, has not some savior, one of the avatars, descended to the darkness of earth?"

"That was a sensible question," said Shri gladly. "Certainly he has come. Holy writings have prophesied his appearance innumerable times, just as Christ was foretold. Wise men have begged to be reborn in our dark age to see Krishna's return to earth. But when this savior wandered among us a little more than four hundred years ago, he performed no wonders, killed no demons, and did not raise the dead. But everyone who saw him felt a wave of inconceivable affection for God. He was the hidden avatar of Kaliyuga, the golden avatar."

"What was his name?" asked Alan, very quietly.

"Krishna Chaitanya," replied Shri.

Chapter XII

The Month of Purushottama

The Indian year—Shri's brother-in-law—Bhagavata and its tales of God—The song of victory—Marching women—Krishna

When the first torrents of rain fell, we left the Goddess Arbuda's wet and foggy mountain top and returned to Nasik and Shri's house, which was stronger and had a protecting roof. To Alan's sorrow, he had been obliged to return to America.

The wandering ascetics of India customarily spend eight months of the year on pilgrimages, never staying long in any one place. But they settle in one place when the heavy rains begin, and during this four-month period they may live under a roof and devote themselves entirely to studying the holy writings.

The Indian year is a lunar year. The twelve months are dedicated to the great avatars, but there is also a thirteenth, intercalary month. This month is dedicated to the source of all divine saviors and bears the name Purushottama, "the highest person."

Krishna himself is praised as Purushottama. It is he who sends avatars to save the world until finally he himself enters the circle of saviors. In the same way, the month of Purushottama occurs every leap year. It is particularly dedicated to God, so during this festive month, it is customary in many Brahman homes to read aloud from scripture, beginning to end, in twelve parts.

Shri sat on his cushion on the tiger skin. His permanent secretary and a brother-in-law, a yogi with a long black beard and long hair, sat with me on the mat before him, singing. The songs were in Marathi, the language spoken in the region around Nasik. Most of the songs were very simple. A couple of women sat crouched in a corner, and they joined in the singing. The men marked the rhythm with small hand cymbals and sang one song after another, repeating them constantly without pausing. It made one think of the waves of the ocean.

The yogi then read from a great book in a solemn, singing tone. As an introduction, he invoked Sarasvati, the goddess of speech and wisdom. She is the divine power of Brahma who is one with him. He then invoked Ganesh, who is usually portrayed in the form of an elephant. A small stone or clay statue of him can be seen in niches and above entrances to many houses in India, for Ganesh, son of Maya, is considered the master of happiness and success. He obtains his power by constantly embracing the feet of Krishna.

The yogi prayed that all these high powers, servants and maids of Krishna might live in his thoughts and speech. He took a bronze bowl and let the water in it run out in a circle about him, and caught a few drops in the cup of his right hand. He let the drops fall on the crown of his head and into his mouth while he repeated the mantra to India's seven holy rivers.

Now and again the speaker bowed and reverently touched his forehead to the book.

When he had read the part set for the day, we all rose and sang in chorus, clapping our hands and swinging candles over the table that was strewn with flowers. Pictures of the saviors of the world were displayed there, included one of Jesus Christ.

Nobody had urged me to join in the singing. I took the initiative myself, and it pleased Shri.

The book we read from every evening is one of humanity's mightiest works—the 18,000-stanza *Bhagavat*. This scripture, which discusses the activities and revelations of God, is often the only book in many Indian homes. The *Bhagavat* is not only a wonderful literary work, but a book about life; it is the bread of life, as the Bible has been to some degree in the West.

The work is ascribed to the great Indian wise man Vyasa. He narrates how God descends to free the earth from the power of demons: How, as a fish, he drew the ark with King Satyavrata, the seven wise men, and all the herbs and animals of the earth through the long night of the flood; how he later appeared as a tortoise, a boar, a man with the head of a lion, a man with an axe, as the boy Vaman, as Rama, as Krishna. He describes bygone times and the future of the world, how God shall descend to conquer the Shudra king and become ruler of the earth.

We read the story of how God revealed himself as Krishna and allowed himself to be born in a dark prison cell. Three thousand years before the birth of Christ, a grim king wanted to kill all the newborn children in order to destroy the divine child that was to threaten his power, just like Herod.

During the month of Purushottama, the city of Nasik resounded with music. Crowds waded into the river Godavari, which overflows all its banks in the rainy season. The temples were inundated, and the forks of the river were filled with singing crowds. On the streets and in homes, people danced until late at night, singing the doings of God. The whole city of Nasik resounded with joy.

The air about our house was filled with sounds of singing and marching feet. The sounds came nearer and nearer. All of us ran to the windows. A troop of women marched in a long line through the garden, singing joyously: "Shri Maharaj, jai, jai, jai—Shri Maharaj, victory, victory, victory!"

A crowd of women from Nasik had assembled to honor Shri with religious singing. They marched around the house, following the direction of the sun, then rushed up the steps, and in a short while were all gathered in the great hall. Some of them bore infants in their arms; now and then they left the room to nurse their children. They sat on the floor about Shri and sang with such piercing voices that the walls vibrated, and they kept the rhythm with small metal cymbals. One began, and the others joined in chorus, singing song after song for several hours.

Shri sat quite still. With a radiant, peaceful countenance, he sat in the midst of them and listened to the songs sung in praise of God, and of himself. Like a child, this man who was one of the countless messengers of God, clapped his hands in rhythm with the others.

When the women had left us and I had returned to my room, I heard Shri clap his hands. I ran downstairs. Shri was waiting in his car, and I took my place beside him. In silence we drove out of the city. Far out in the country he motioned for the car to stop. We stepped out, turned off from the road, and entered a wide, newly ploughed field. The sky was covered with heavy banks of clouds, which rose from the horizon and towered up as far as one could see.

"The earth wishes to be fructified," Shri remarked slowly. After a while he pointed once more to the darkening sky and mumbled, "Krishna, Krishna."

I knew what Shri meant. The Sanskrit word "Krishna" means not only the god Krishna, but also the nimbus blue or violet, almost black color of a thundercloud that is heavy with rain.

PART TWO
THE CAMP IN INDIA

CHAPTER XIII

"SHIVA WILL CALL YOU"

Peace in the guru's house—A rude awakening—Behind the barbed wire—Indian prison camps—Mutual suspicions—The apes look on, astonished—Prison politics—Petty irritations of prison life—The hospital haven—Hovering vultures—The song of the peasants

I lived peacefully in my teacher's house in Nasik. Rosebushes bloomed in the garden almost year-round, and every morning I picked a big bunch and placed them here and there in Shri's meditation room.

Shri had several times expressed a definite wish that I should not read the newspapers. My progress on the spiritual path along which he was leading me could be disturbed by my reading them. He saw, of course, that current events were upsetting me, and I understood that it was wisest to obey him. However, when at times I could not repress my anxiety for my wife and child in Austria, he assured me that they were protected. To calm my fears, he kindly invited my family to live as his children at his house in Nasik. We had already begun discussing which school in India my boy should attend. It took a lot of trouble to get permission for my wife and child—Shanti and Gunananda, as Shri called them—to enter India, but the official approval finally arrived.

Europe was far away. Far off, too, were the mighty Himalayas, the northern boundary of India, where I had never gone farther than the first ridges. I asked my guru many times, "Shri, when shall we take up the interrupted pilgrimage to Shiva's home?"

The old man smiled in a strange way. "Wait until the time comes. *Shiva will call you!*"

I longed for the great forests, the lonely lakes, and the uninhabited mountain slopes where Shiva is enthroned in the wilderness. At night, I often dreamed that I lay again on the rough boards of one of the humble pilgrim shelters, rank smoke from an open fire in the room below penetrating the cracks in the floor. The coolies, hired to bear Shri's palanquin to Lake Manasarovar, were preparing their meagre meal down there. Shiva's portrait hung on the rough, white-washed stone walls of the house.

This portrait depicted Shiva lost in meditation. He sat rigid, his legs crossed under him, his naked body smeared with the white ash of cremated bodies. The snakes intertwined around his arms represented the snake-like desires of the sensual world that stretched after him. But Shiva did not notice the snakes and their lively tongues. He gazed into a kingdom not of this world. Below the portrait were the words, "Shiva meditating on Krishna."

I once came across another color print of Shiva in a bazaar, and I hung it on the wall of my peaceful room at Anandapith. Here a youthful Shiva was depicted as the destroyer. He danced with ecstasy in the empty spaces above a dismally burning world, crushing it under his strides. He danced in order to make room for a new creation.

One morning, when it was quite early and still dark outside, I awoke out of a sound sleep. I thought I heard the roar of thunder. Down below someone was knocking impatiently with fists or the butt of a gun on the door of Shri's house. But Shri had gone to Rana's house for a few days. I heard the door open. Heavy footsteps, like those of shoes shod with iron, stomped up the wooden stairs. A uniformed police inspector and a group of Indian soldiers entered my room.

"You are arrested. Get ready immediately. Take only the most necessary things with you. And come along, for war has broken out."

While I was dressing as hastily as I could, they poked about in my dresser and my trunk. When I finished, they pushed me into a waiting car. We drove through the familiar landscape, where I had driven so many times sitting beside Shri in his car. This time an Indian soldier sat on each side of me, and one sat beside the chauffeur. All of them had loaded guns with fixed bayonets. The car stopped in front of a gate that had a high, barbed-wire fence, and to my amazement I recalled that a little over two decades ago, as a young soldier in the First World War, I had stood on guard outside an exactly similar barbed-wire entrance. This had been in Austria, where I was stationed as guard outside a camp for Russian prisoners of war.

Now I was being led as a prisoner into the camp, through the outer and the inner gates of the barbed-wire enclosures, double fencing, and into a barrack where a few drowsy people sat waiting. During the course of the day, several hundred people were led into the prison camp, transported by car and by train. Since I had come to India on an Austrian passport, the war had caused me to become a so-called "enemy alien" overnight. Hundreds of thousands had met the same fate: confinement in prison camps surrounded by barbed wire.

While Shiva danced, the earth trembled and thousand-year-old empires fell like packs of cards. People all over the world were building mighty fortifications to retain their various systems, which all had something in common: retaliation and revenge. New camps were being built—and filled—in all parts of the world: in Africa and Asia, in America and Australia, in Europe and naturally in India, too. Day and night the work went on, in the glowing heat of the sun, and by searchlight. In nearly every country and at unbelievable expense, ugly barracks covered with tiles, or thatch, or corrugated iron, were set up. When traveling by train, there were long stretches where one saw nothing but barracks, one after the other. Great forests were chopped down to procure enough wood for the prison camps that were needed. Thousands of freight cars and hundreds of shiploads of barbed wire were unloaded, unrolled and quickly stretched out, twisted together into impenetrable prickly hedges of sharp wire. Grain fields were leveled and fruit trees cut to clear space for prison camps.

The Indian camps in which I spent about six years of my life were tolerable. There were no gas chambers, no flogging or torture cells, no ovens for burning human beings. They could in no way be compared with the concentration camps in Germany and neighboring countries. The simple fare was generally good and sufficient. Naturally, it consisted almost exclusively of meat preparations, and during the latter years mainly of canned foods. It was not the fault of the authorities that many of those who were interned suffered from a lack of vitamins and lost their teeth; there was famine in many parts of India. It was my own fault that I sometimes starved, for I was obstinate in my determination to retain my vegetarian diet. In spite of the good treatment, however, no one in the camp escaped being at times overcome by despair.

Those in power in all parts of the world tried to be as all-seeing as God himself. An ingenious system of secret police looked about with a hundred thousand searching eyes and listened with a hundred thousand listening ears. This ghost-like monster had sense organs and clutching arms that stretched over the world and reached into the prison camps.

As soon as I became established in the Indian prison camp, I began to receive whispered information. "Watch out. Be careful. That person is being friendly only in order to pump you for information. He is a spy, a Nazi agent. That one? He writes reports for the English. He admitted this himself once while drunk. And I saw him with my own eyes leaving a report to the sergeant early one morning. And that one? My God! Don't you know that he is a communist? He belongs to G.P.U. Don't you believe that the Russians have their confidants here in the camp, among both Nazis and anti-Nazis?"

Anguish tore at this web of a few thousand human beings.

Great hordes of gray and brown apes hovered outside the camp. They were led by a very old he-ape, a very despotic dictator. There were often a great many of these animals, young and old, male and female, just outside the outer, barbed-wire fence of the enclosure.

They all stared with sad, serious eyes at the strange world of humans behind the bars.

Sometimes we laughed at the sight. "Things are splendid here—we even have a zoological garden!" But then we realized the truth. The apes outside were free, watching us caged humans.

What did they see?

The apes saw human beings digging in the earth, planting banana trees and other trees as well. The humans arranged small gardens in front of their barracks. They watered the garden beds. They planted flowers and vegetables. They worked at carpentry, or laid pipes, hammered nails, forged, and welded. They mixed cement, built with tiles and stones, and waged war against lice in their beds and holes in their clothes. They played cards and let the worn-out gramophone spin for hours at a time. They talked, quarreled, fought. Many lay all day idling on their barrack beds that crawled with lice, each and every one imprisoned in a nightmare.

Each of the camp's eight different enclosures had its own self-government. A regular national-socialistic state existed behind the carefully guarded outer wall. There were leaders, assistant leaders, and an inner circle. There was a Nazi organization for *Kraft durch Freude*, and associations for sport and athletic contests and for music, theatricals, and instruction. Whoever wished could work at his education, whether it was the first principles in writing, a course in some trade or an examination test. But there were also blacklists, secret papers, boycotts of undesirable elements, conversion of opposing groups, punishment by flogging, attempts to censure letters and Gestapo.

Nearby, in the wing for anti-Nazis and anti-fascists, a strictly democratic system prevailed, with regular voting and violent election campaigns. There they prayed openly in many languages, that the Allies would be victorious. People in this section lived constantly as if they sat in a waiting room: Only a few days more, a few weeks, "until the application is granted." All waited for their prompt release. Many of them waited for more than seven years. Behind the barbed-wire fence they celebrated the victory at the close of the war, and then had to continue waiting for years, in bitterness and mortification.

In another barbed-wire enclosure were Italian Catholic missionaries, including two bishops. This was a real pontifical state in miniature, two hundred and fifty yards wide and three hundred long.

There was also a section for about a hundred Italian generals who had been taken prisoner in East Africa. They were divided into a fascist and an anti-fascist group, the two of them passionately fighting each other. One evening a crowd of prisoners stood up against the wire fence of one of the enclosures, and, facing the neighboring enclosure inimically, shrieked as they beat rhythmically in a talking chorus: "Du-cé! Du-cé! Du-cé! Du-cé!...Hit-ler! Hit-ler! Hit-ler! Hit-ler!" In the other enclosure, anti-Fascists hanged a life-size effigy of Mussolini in the glow of a burning fire to the accompaniment of wild acclamation, as if they had a preconception of coming events. Just as the swinging dictator was about to be lowered from the gallows and cast into the flames—this took place long after midnight—the English sergeant came marching in with a number of guards. He was stern and abrupt, and had been given the name "Nutcracker." His false teeth gnashed threateningly, but he asked in a friendly tone, "Who is the artist? Who made this excellent arrangement?"

Flattered, the arrangers reported themselves—and were promptly led away under guard to the prison barrack, since they were disturbers of the peace. Violent exclamations of indignation flowed from their comrades, and expressions of approval from the opponents on the other side of the fence.

We were given the best possible care. We even enjoyed a large cinema barrack—within the barbed wire, of course, but with electric fans to counteract the heat. The cinema was open also to members of the European guard and to the officers. When this barrack burnt down, it was rebuilt within a few weeks. The work went on day and night, for the Indian agent did not want to be deprived of this income. We marched to the cinema in three columns, under escort, out through the double fencing of our enclosures. The Nazis marched in step, and as a sign of protest the anti-Nazis walked out of step. Irritated by the disturbance, the apes climbed up into the leafage of the trees and bared their teeth. And there we sat, tightly packed, enveloped in the pungent smoke of innumerable cheap cigarettes, watching worn-out American sensational films. We saw news films, too; a young queen distributed flowers and sweets among wounded soldiers; noisy squadrons dropped giant bombs that dug gigantic craters in the earth, and before our eyes destroyed great cities—our hometowns, perhaps—in minutes.

Life in the strictly isolated prison camp was just as it was outside. All the problems, all the agony, the piercing pain, and the hate easily penetrated the double barbed-wire fence, to believers and unbelievers, Jews, Catholics, Protestants, and followers of all imaginable Christian beliefs; to citizens of about twenty European countries (Estonians, Lithuanians, Finns, Bulgarians, Rumanians, Hungarians, Germans, Austrians, and Italians) and also to imprisoned citizens of Allied countries (Czechs, Poles, Greeks, Danes, Norwegians, Dutch, Russians). All of them had been taken unaware by the war somewhere in the wide-stretching lands or the flowering islands between New Guinea and Iraq, and between Hong Kong and Abyssinia, and now they had been assembled into one great camp in India.

All of them tried to continue their lives as they had been before the war. Some even retained their titles as directors or education councils. Many had been managers or owners of immense plantations with fantastic incomes, and had moved in influential circles. Trunks were unpacked at regular intervals—at least those that had not sunk to the bottom of the sea. One ship transporting prisoners from a Dutch camp in Sumatra had been sunk by a Japanese U-boat. All the prisoners' property was heaped outdoors, and dinner clothes were aired in the sun to protect them from moths. Dinner jackets and swallow-tails hung on clothes lines and waved about importantly in the breeze. Now and again one of the internees could be seen promenading on a Sunday afternoon between the barracks and the latrines in his dinner suit and starched white shirt, just to feel like a gentleman for an hour or two. Then the clothes were laid in camphor again, and the khaki shorts were resumed.

Memories were unpacked but never locked up. Each year passed, the present became more and more empty, and hopes built on hollow phrases fell like packs of cards. Thousands of prisoners lived passionately in the past; they reveled in it. For hours and days they walked up and down the length of the wire fencing and talked about what they had once eaten at such and such restaurant, describing in detail the items on the menu and the carefully chosen wines, and what sensations they had enjoyed at the taste of them. In the same way, they told of their experiences with women, of good and bad business deals, of how they had given this or that person what he deserved. They eagerly sought new friends who had not heard their stories and witticisms. New arrivals from other camps were immediately surrounded by people who wanted to talk about their past. Many prisoners avoided one another, nauseated by the many years of living together in the same barrack. They could not tolerate the other's nearness, his stories, his way of laughing.

Some of the internees had domestic pets. They built small cages within their own cages for their pets, and they gave these animals all their affection. One man, who boasted of helping set fire to synagogues in Germany, affectionately looked after his captive parrots, titmice, nightingales, and other birds. A kindly German musician, a strong anti-Nazi, tamed mice for a hobby. He once placed a lost field mouse in a cage with a mouse family. The tiny stranger, a female, cautiously crept into a corner of the cage, but the all the mice caught her smell. They were irritated and threatened by her presence. Evidently the mice considered the shivering little stranger a treacherous intruder. Half an hour later the stranger, probably of another species, lay dead in a pool of blood, bitten to death by sharp teeth.

Undoubtedly, the best place in the whole camp was the hospital. This hospital was open to all the different hostile parties, yet it was only there that one could really find peace. When the patients suffered from pain, their fanatical faces could often reassume a kindly human expression, like those of children. Oh, how many strange fates were revealed to me when old men and young, who had spent decades in the tropics, related their life stories while lying in the hospital during a sleepless night just before or after a serious operation, or in the face of approaching death. They were so grateful for the slightest intimation of kindness that they forgot that a person of another party or race lay in the next bed. But as soon as they recovered or felt a glimmer of hope, their faces could become hard and scornful, and they resumed boycotting or secretly reporting their companions.

The camp churchyard lay in a separate section and was not enclosed by barbed wire. The graves were looked after carefully and were decorated with flowers by the interned, who were escorted there under guard. But mutual contempt did not halt even in the face of death. The strongest party in the camp complained that their dead were outraged by the burial of members of the opposing party in the same graveyard, so the camp commander felt obliged to have anti-Nazis, anti-Fascists, and Jews buried far away, in the next city.

On the roof of the kitchen barracks, in all eight sections of the prison camp, sat ugly vulture-like birds of prey, crowded into rows. They were the real masters of the camp. No barbed wire held them back, no guards shot at them as they swooped in over the fences and pried into the various groups of human beings. What did these birds see? They saw booty. It did not matter to them whether their prey was an anti-Fascist, a Fascist, or a Catholic priest who left the kitchen barrack with a tin plate that had just been filled. The birds swooped down in wild swarms and seized pieces of meat. In their eagerness they sometimes aimed poorly, and an ugly, bloody wound appeared on the hand bearing the plate.

The prison camp was a throbbing bit of life beneath the feet of Shiva the Destroyer, surrounded on all sides by the vast country of India. On its winding dusty roads, as everywhere between Himalaya and Cape Comorin, the ox-carts of Indian farmers rolled in endless columns in the gray hours preceding daybreak. The song of the farmers rose and fell in monotones. It was as if the whole world longed for daybreak, begging that the spiritual sun might rise over the night-enveloped earth:

> The mighty Godhead, born in distant aeons,
> eternal, pristine, timeless, all-embracing,
> streams down from every morning sunbeam
> and gazes from all creatures blessed with vision...
> the wise, the ageless, ever-youthful Atman.

Chapter XIV

Imprisoned–Free–Imprisoned

Trying to meditate in prison—Messages from Shri—Committees decide fate of prisoners—In a women's camp—Unexpectedly set free—With Shri in Mahabaleshvar—Banquet in Shri's honor—The Germans enter Paris—Back to prison—The jackals laugh at a mad world

Within the barracks of the camp, I tried to continue living as I had lived with my guru, with daily meditation. I shut myself off egotistically. There were a few single rooms in the camp, and for a while my only aim was to obtain one of these rooms, to work there undisturbed and to meditate. At least I might find a corner in one of the barracks. This would mean that I had a bed on only one side of me and a protecting wall on the other. The *Bhagavad-gita* asks, "How can one find peace without meditation?"

I decided to try to meditate in the midst of the noise and the crowd, my legs crossed under me as I sat on my bed—and naturally, I was laughed at. There were often twenty of us taking a shower at the same time, and the water could be shut off just as we stood there lathered from top to toe. At such times I sang the sacred syllable AUM quietly to myself, forgetful of my surroundings. I meditated on the ancient word whose three sounds signify the creation, maintenance, and destruction of the world, the three phases of time (past, present and future), and the occult that knows no time. This irritated my comrades.

Sometimes, I would come across a neglected place in a corner of the camp, behind a rabbit hutch or a hen coop, where I could meditate in solitude. Still glowing from my meditation, I often went directly to the long queue in front of the kitchen barrack, from which generally emanated sounds like those made by a crowd of hungry beasts waiting for food. Someone once shouted to me angrily, "Why do you always go about smiling like a Mona Lisa? I can't understand how anyone could smile in such a situation as ours."

I had not yet grasped that the external requirements of meditation—the mat of kusha grass (which, by the way, was stolen on my very first day in the camp), the separate room, and solitude—are requirements for a beginner.

The walls I tried to build around me in the camp soon caved in. The white mosquito net that we stretched over our beds at night gave me a kind of seclusion. But it might happen that some drunk I had unwittingly offended tore away the net in the middle of the night to beat me and shower me with foul language.

"Be passionless, calm, peaceful. Bestow on those around you your own calm, your peace, your strength!" Thus had Shri written to me when the authorities finally gave us permission to correspond.

I was horrified when I read these words from Shri. I had lived as if part of my being had become numbed. I had been goaded about, and I allowed myself to be like a puppet tied to a string. A shrill whistle woke me in the morning. Shrill whistling summoned me to the athletic field for the daily roll call. A whistle called me to potato peeling and other duties. I had to polish windows or wash floors. Someone shouted to me, and in turn I shouted to others. Where was my real self?

When I try to recall the first days of my imprisonment, I only remember moving from one enclosure to another, from barrack to tent, tent to barrack. As soon as I began to feel at home, I could be sure of getting an order to move. My comrades and I moved our belongings from one part of the camp to another innumerable times. Sometimes the whole camp moved. Once, we traveled in a long column of buses to new barracks. In the middle of a desert steppe, all the cars stopped suddenly, and we were ordered to get out. We were driven into a great square made up of soldiers who stood close to each other. Aiming their loaded guns at us, they commanded us to perform our physical needs. When this command had been obeyed, we re-entered the buses and drove on to the next camp, where we had no more peace than before.

Meanwhile, inspection committees at the camps were deciding which of the interned could be freed. The committees weighed the case of each prisoner in the large camp, a smaller camp high up in Himalaya near Darjeeling, camps to the south in the Nilgiri mountains, and a women's camp in the Deccan. I was sent there for a few weeks by mistake—or was it some kind of joke?

No barbed wire was to be seen there. The barracks were placed on beautiful lawns, filling the spaces between groups of aged trees. European women wandered about under the trees, many of them young and handsome, dressed in light summer dresses, trousers or shorts. Some of them lay stretched out on deck chairs, and waved at me with gay parasols as I drove up to the encampment in a bus, guarded by three soldiers. A beautiful river glittered nearby, resembling "Fagervik" (Heiterbucht) in Strindberg's drama *Traumspiel*.

In this camp, lipstick and other cosmetics were sold in the canteen, and dining tables were decorated with white tablecloths and flowers. But the prisoners were also divided into narrow cages by invisible barbed wire. The German women refused to sit at the same table as Jewesses or Aryan women married to Jews. These hostile factions dined at different hours and boycotted one another. The Italian and German women dined together, but even they boycotted each other and did not converse. The respectable Italian women and the Italian prostitutes from Bombay avoided and despised each other heartily. Hostile groups exchanged hateful glances from the four corners of the assembly room. Charming young creatures used every means to fashion intrigue and disparage one another before the commandant and the investigating commission. Though at first glance the camp appeared to resemble "Fagervik," it was rather "Skamsund" (Schmachsund). Many of these women wept secretly at night over the rumors whispered about them. A few went insane.

When, after a short stay, I re-entered the bus that was to take me back to my former camp, women from these different groups crowded about it. All of them, both those who had scorned me and those who had been friendly, begged me to promise to take messages to their imprisoned husbands, some of them in departments that I had no possibility of entering. Even when the wheels of the heavy, worn vehicle had begun grating on the sand, they entreated me to beg their husbands to try every means possible to reunite them.

The committees worked for months. When one left, a new one came. Every prisoner had to fill out a questionnaire and was called in repeatedly for cross-examination. Witnesses were questioned; all accusations were written down. The reports of the secret police on each person were investigated thoroughly. Judgment was passed on everybody.

One day, quite unexpectedly, I was given my freedom.

Amazed, I went through the barbed-wire gate into the open. The next day I was once again at Shri's home, and the old man took me in his arms.

The great prison camp, where hundreds of my comrades sat behind double iron bars, soon vanished from my thoughts like a dream. At times I was surprised at being able to go where I wished, and that nowhere was there any barbed wire to hinder me. I soon left the hot plains, accompanying Shri up to the wooded mountain regions of Mahabaleshvar. We lived there by ourselves in a tiny house. An ancient Krishna temple rose nearby on the edge of a precipice, and I often sat in the cold hall of the temple at the foot of a statue. It represented Krishna, the divine boy, as he grew up among the shepherds of Brindaban, walking through the forest and playing a flute. A clear spring welled forth at the foot of the statue. It gushed down the slope, becoming on the plains the wide river that somewhere in the dim distance flowed past the women's encampment.

Rana came and visited us, and just as before, we sat at Shri's feet and he interpreted the Upanishads for us. The old man was as happy as a child, and most of the time he smiled easily. But when he explained the secret teachings of the Upanishads, his words were like flashes of lightning; it seemed as if the firmament stood aglow over us, and as if eternity, void of time and space, was revealed to us.

Every morning I arose before sunrise, and after a hasty bath climbed a hill, where I meditated. During the first months the skies of spring and summer were cloudless as I opened my eyes after meditation. Gradually the signs of a new rainy season period gathered over the forests. When I opened my eyes and looked about in astonishment, mighty banks of clouds and thick mists rushed up the crevices. Clouds heavy with rain enveloped the earth. It would soon be time to leave the mountain plateau, with its great forests and heavy-scented orchids growing on the mossy branches of the trees. The first showers had already come. The booming of thunder sounded in the distance. Poisonous snakes had begun to creep out of their water-filled holes in the earth. Flashes of rumors about the results of the German offensive in Norway and in the West reached our peaceful little home through Shri's servant, who shopped in the bazaars of the village every week, an hour's journey away. An official notice reached us, too. The permission for my wife and child to enter the country, which had already been granted and renewed, was suddenly revoked. A guest from the city reported that foreigners of hostile nationality that had been freed were being re-arrested.

Shortly before our departure, the Brahmans in the little temple village of Mahabaleshvar held a banquet in honor of Shri. We drove the short distance to the gaily decorated house to which we had been invited in Shri's elegant eight-cylinder Ford, a gift from one of his Indian pupils. The old priest, who many years ago had performed the marriage rites for one of Shri's daughters, seemed embarrassed when he received us. It appeared that some of the more orthodox Brahmans in the village did not want to eat at the same table as a

European. They wanted me to eat my meal on the adjacent veranda, apart from the other guests.

Shri disagreed with them. He explained that I was his pupil, and that as my guru he had bestowed on me the Brahman cord and accepted me as a Brahman. They discussed deeply and lengthily, without reaching a decision. We returned hungry to our little house.

In my stupidity, I was very proud of the fact that Shri had not failed me or allowed them to treat me like a barbarian. I did not suspect that without wasting words on the matter, he criticized my behavior. As my teacher, he had intervened on behalf of his pupil. But my immediate reaction should have been to willingly declare that I should be glad to dine out on the veranda. I had learned nothing during my imprisonment. I had not yet been granted the gift of humility.

The next day we left the mountain village.

As we approached the plains, people seemed to be more and more excited. The Germans had marched into Paris and were spreading out over France. The most fantastic rumors were being spread and believed. "Whatever happens, you must preserve your inner calm," Shri advised me. I tried, but succeeded only partially. Shortly after our arrival at Nasik, the familiar figure of the police inspector appeared with his followers, and a new order of arrest was presented. Under heavy guard, I and hundreds of others who had been given their freedom were taken back to the camp surrounded by barbed wire. My fleeting freedom had been only a short vacation from imprisonment.

Once again I lay in the stuffy barrack, under a white mosquito net, among crowds of people who groaned under the ruins of their broken-down pasts, and who were full of fears for the future. I could not sleep. I could not banish the pictures that appeared behind the lids of my closed eyes. Like the others, I was filled with anxiety. I could not quell my fears for my family, my mother, my wife and my child. They were still in Austria, where the dangers were increasing daily. Perhaps they were already in a prison camp much worse than mine. I could not worrying about my own fate and the grief that my spiritual training was for the second time interrupted (apparently, without reason). I sat up in bed and meditated, as Shri had taught me. But when I lay down again, tired after the strain, the painful pictures reappeared and remained before my eyes, and my thoughts rolled on in their obligatory tracks. It was like being in a world of ghosts.

My neighbors groaned and turned restlessly in their sleep, so that the beds were creaking. Often the barrack was filled with moaning, as if the sleepers were in a nightmare.

Outside the camp, jackals were shrieking. I could not sleep. A painful picture kept returning: All the people in the prison camp— no, all the people in the world—lay at the bottom of a dark prison hole. All of us were bound, bound by the chains of our own desire, our own prejudice, bound by our ignorance, by our lack of humility. I thought of a metaphor from some ancient book, though I couldn't recall which one. Plato, perhaps? The prisoners in the dark cave all stared in the same direction, eyes filled with anguish. We watched a play of shadows on a flickering wall. We saw only the dance of the distorted shadows, which we could not understand. But the living figures in the realm of reality, only the shadows of which fell into the cave, could not be discerned; they were hidden from us.

I covered my eyes to chase away the picture. I longed for a few drops of water, and got up to go to the well and drink. I went quietly, so as not to wake those who slept, walking in the darkness between the rows of beds toward the door of the long, narrow barrack.

Outside, the cries of the jackals around the camp sounded even more shrill. Soon the chorus quieted down, and only one animal continued his shrieking. It sounded like an ever-increasing roar of laughter, an insane laugh at the strange world in which we lived.

CHAPTER XV

THE FEAST OF THE UNTOUCHABLES

The latrine cleaners and their guru—The story of Valmiki, the fallen Brahman—Drums in the night—Singing soldiers—I pray for a guru

I sat with my legs crossed on the empty football field, beyond the black sleeping barracks. In the daytime this place was filled with life and motion, vibrating with the tread of two teams and the cheers of the onlookers. Now silence reigned, and the prisoners slept heavily.

Singing could be heard in the distance. It came from the ugly, narrow quarters of the latrine cleaners. These men cleaned the many latrine barrels of the big camp with their hands and the help of short brooms. A crowd of happy people moved around a big outdoor fire. A red banner, lighted up by the flames, waved in the wind from a tall pole in front of their barracks. This was the sign that their Valmiki-guru had arrived. That was why they were celebrating.

These Indians, who performed the most menial cleaning jobs for the camp, were thoroughly despised by the prisoners behind the barbed-wire fence. All the race superiority of the white man made its appearance in connection with these colored people, who were often only a shade darker in complexion than those who looked down on them. This was the only point on which the Jewish intellectual and the Nazi could agree at times. Even those who were persecuted in their own homeland because of their race, despised these Indian servants. In the camp they were seldom called anything other than blacks and niggers. Innumerable times I heard, "That damned sweeper should have a flogging." "Quite right, Mr. Colleague."

But even these despised people had their guru, who helped them interpret life according to their present circumstances, and who gave them instruction in spiritual matters. In India the path to the highest goal is never closed to any person; even thieves and prostitutes have had their own gurus for thousands of years.

The latrine cleaner is often too poor to satisfy his hunger, let alone to buy a bit of soap. In the beating torrents of the monsoon, perhaps he has nothing but an old ragged sack to cover his thin, naked shoulders. But yet he can have a rough conception of the fact that within himself exists an eternal atman, which wanders through the ages. He knows that he has brought about his hard fate in this life through his deeds in a former existence and that his behavior in this life determines his destiny. This teaching is known only to a few of the most profound mystics of the West: "All creatures have existed eternally in the divine essence....all beings *were*, before their creation, one with the essence of God." Yet it is understood by many an Indian latrine cleaner. As Krishna says in the *Bhagavad-gita*, "Never was there a time when I, nor thou, nor these lords of men, were not, nor will there ever be a time hereafter, when we shall cease to be.... As a man throweth away old garments and putteth on new; even so, the soul in the body, having quitted its old mortal frame, entereth into others which are new....The weapon divideth it not, the fire burneth it not, the water corrupteth it not, the wind drieth it not away; for it is indivisible, inconsumable, incorruptible....Therefore, knowing it to be thus, thou shouldst not grieve."

This ancient wisdom of man, almost forgotten in the West, is well-known to the Hindus, to those who steer their cars through the crowds of great tropical cities or speculate on the exchange overcome by desire for gain, and sometimes to the despised people who perform the most menial jobs for the white sahibs in a concentration camp.

But none of my fellow prisoners were interested in the existence of an eternal Atman.

I looked through the barbed wire toward the barracks of the coolies. They sat in the glow of the fire around the Valmiki-guru and listened to his words. I was reminded of the story of Valmiki, whose name is borne by casteless spiritual teachers. He, too, was once despised by all, and his story is of great comfort to all those who have fallen into the depths of despair, believing they can never rise again.

He who acquired the name Valmiki was originally a fallen Brahman. In ancient India, a Brahman who lost his caste was looked upon as lower than the lowest, casteless person. This outcast had become a highway robber out of sheer defiance, and he murdered and plundered travelers who passed through the thick forest where he lived in a dark cave.

A seer once wandered through this forest. He had no longer any personal feeling for gain or loss on earth. In his boundless sympathy for man, he wandered about in search of souls that were worthy of receiving the greatest treasure: *bhakti*, affectionate devotion to God.

The robber rushed out of the thick brush to kill and plunder the wanderer. He expected to find treasures on him. Swinging his club over the head of the old man, he was amazed at the bright smile and the child-like innocence reflected there. He hesitated. "My son, why should you commit such a great crime?" asked the intended victim mildly, and without any sign of fear.

The club fell from the hand of the grim robber. He threw himself before the traveler and touched his forehead to the man's naked foot. Then he lifted his ravaged face, which was wet with tears, and said with a sigh, "O great holy one, I see now what I am. You have illuminated the unbelievable darkness of my life. Oh, give me a holy mantra that can wash away the horrible dirt of my sins."

"Yes, my son, I shall do so," said the wise man. He bent down lovingly over the man who lay on the ground at his feet, until his lips reached the ear of the robber. "Repeat this mantra," he whispered. "Sing the two syllables that form the name of God: Ra-ma, Ra-ma, Ra-ma…"

The robber cried out with fright. "Not that word! Not that word! Oh, my father, how could I let my sullied lips utter the name of God?"

The rishi smiled. "My child, repeat the syllables in reverse order. Sing: Ma-ra, ma-ra, ma-ra....You know what that means?"

The robber sighed. "Yes, I know what that word means: Death. Yes, that is the right word for me."

The devotee of God laid his hand in blessing on the sinner's head. The robber dried his eyes, sat on the ground with his legs crossed, back rigid and his head raised. He closed his eyes half way and directed his gaze to the tip of his nose, and sang, "Ma-ra, ma-ra, ma-ra...death, death, death..."

Many years later the same rishi passed through the same forest, stopping at the place where he had once performed initiation for the robber. He looked around. Only an ant hill rose on one side of the path. The rishi looked closer, and to his surprise saw that a man's eyes and hair stuck out of the ant hill. A man sat there motionless in the pose for meditation. He sat so still that the ants had built their dwelling over him undisturbed. Lost in deep rapture, only his lips moved. Almost noiselessly he was singing: "Rama, Rama, Rama..."

The Sanskrit word for ant hill is *valmiki*. The fallen Brahman, the abhorred robber, has been praised for thousands of years now as the holy man and poet Valmiki, composer of the epic Ramayana, a bottomless ocean of stories about God when He wandered the earth under the name Rama.

While Valmiki had unceasingly repeated the two syllables ma-ra, ma-ra, ma-ra, they had automatically changed into Rama, Rama, Rama....God, God, God. The power of God's name had washed all the dirt from Valmiki's soul, and had enabled him to look into the kingdom of God and understand his descent to earth.

"Like wonderful, life-giving streams flowing in every direction from a great, inexhaustible lake, the divine saviors descend from God eternally. Just as innumerable sparks stream in every direction from a great fire, the great avatars depart eternally from God's ancient fire, the fire of love. In order to redeem, they descend upon the earth and other worlds, remove the burdens of these worlds, and then return to their origin, the fire." Thus it is written in the holy scriptures of India.

The great fire of the untouchables rose into the night. It is not only the casteless, but God, too, who is called *Untouchable.* Clear sparks flew from the fire. Rejoicing, the latrine cleaners arose when their guru, illumined by the light of the fire, stood up and began to sing. In ecstasy, he began to describe God's love, God's doings, his eternal acts of devotion in all the worlds and towards all beings, high and low, humans and animals. The coolies rejoiced and danced around their teacher and around the fire. As the whirl of happy people moved in the firelight, their voices rose in chorus. "Krishna! Krishna! Krishna!" They beat Shiva's drum and sang the name of the hidden God on whom Shiva meditates continually with a blissful smile, entwined with snakes, smeared with ashes of the dead, burnt by the poison of the world of senses.

The peasants in a Hindu village on the south border of the encampment had also lit a fire. They beat on Shiva's drum too and danced around a fire, rejoicing as they sang, "Krishna, Krishna!"

Is there some great Krishna festival today? I wondered. I had no almanac with me in which the festivals of the Hindus were listed.

Even the Indian guards, who marched to and fro tirelessly in the barbed-wire entrance, marched tonight with almost dancing steps, singing "Krishna, Krishna, Krishna."

Out of the dark doorway of one of the barracks came a shower of foul words. "Shut up with that whining! You swine! You dirty cattle! You damned niggers! Shut up right away!" To give strength to their slumber, they threw out an empty tin can, which scraped angrily on the cement outside the barrack. It was as if a stinking stream of manure water had run out into the night.

Frightened and worried over having been the cause of complaint from the imprisoned white sahibs, the Indian soldiers immediately ceased their song to God and returned quietly to their march between the two barbed-wire fences.

With a heavy heart I sat down on the athletic field of the camp. I felt as if a fog had settled over me.

I thought of my old mother who lived in the Jewish quarter of Vienna, frightened and insulted by people like those who had just shrieked from the barracks. I saw her before me, the old, worn face under the snow white hair, and the blue eyes that had gazed so long after me as I drove to the station on my departure to India. I heard again her brave words of farewell: "We two belong to each other, even if we are separated outwardly."

I thought of my wife and my child. Had they escaped the firm persecution of the Jews? Or had they been sent to some camp in Poland? Were they still alive? Information seldom reached us, and then months late, through the double filters of censorship.

I thought of my guru, Shri Maharaj, who had not received permission to visit me at the camp. He had been willing to make a long and troublesome journey to see me for a few minutes, in the presence of an officer. But he was not allowed to come; only in a few exceptional cases was a short visit permitted for some close relative. And yet Shri was more to me than a father. Everyone who truly desired so, even the untouchables, could be near their guru. But not I.

The joy and trust that lay deep down in my heart refused to allow anything to discourage me, however.

The fires were still burning. Crowds of coolies danced and sang in the bright glow of the firelight. They cried, "Krishna, Krishna, Krishna!" The peasants in the village on the south side of the camp still beat their drums and danced about the fire rejoicing: "Krishna, Krishna, Krishna." The marching guards had also begun singing again: "Krishna, Krishna Krishna!"

"O thou hidden God to whom all turn…O thou God, of whom I know nothing—let me stand the test. Send me a helper, a guru, that I may learn what I have thus far neglected to learn of life: love." Thus my heart prayed in the night.

PART THREE

SADANANDA

CHAPTER XVI

My Friend Sadananda

*The coming of Sadananda—The path to the forgotten world—First talk
with my new guru—The meaning of "The Friend of the Lordless"—
Questions that should not be asked*

When I prayed to God for a guru, one was already very near. One
day there stood a newcomer outside the kitchen barrack, where a
hungry crowd had gathered and the birds of prey circled overhead
in eager swarms. He was tall and slender, and his head was shaved.
Although he was European, he wore the gown of an Indian monk.
His name was Sadananda.

I spoke to him, and he answered in a matter-of-fact way with
monosyllables. Our first real conversation took place at night on the
football field. There he told me about an antique Greek vase he had
once seen. The decoration on it was a wheel with sixteen spokes, and
around the wheel were pictures from the ancient Greek mysteries
and the inscription, "I have jumped off the wheel of Ixion."

According to the conception of the ancient Greeks, Ixion
was a man loaded with misdeeds, who was bound after death for all
eternity to a wheel that turned incessantly—I remembered that
much. But I had not grasped the fact that the Greek mysteries refer
to our world as the place of misery, where every living being is
bound without knowing it to a turning wheel, the wheel of repeated existences on earth.

I happened to think of a wheel in an old, abandoned mill that
I used to stare at for hours at a time in my childhood. Its spokes
were covered with gray moss. It turned round in a dark crevice

whose walls were black with age and cast up the water of the stream in cascades, which immediately fell and dispersed again: gain and loss, honor and ignominy, victory and defeat, joy and sorrow, health and illness, meeting and parting, death and rebirth. The force of personal desire was the water of the stream, which endlessly drives the wheel in the world of change. All the wisdom of India strives to free mankind from this wheel of Ixion. Shri, too, considered this delivery to be the highest goal.

"Delivery from the fire of suffering in the world of change is not the highest goal," said my companion. "That delivery is only the first step on the infinite path that leads into God's *forgotten world*, the path on which the guru who loves God leads his disciple."

"What kind of a path is that? What is the goal?" I asked expectantly.

"The path is love, the goal is love, ever greater, ever more heartfelt love of God. Just as it is the nature of fire to burn, so it is the nature of the human soul to love God. Just as a spark is evidence of a fire, because it is burning, the soul is evidence of God, because it loves. The spark is the single soul, the great fire of love is God. The spark is little and insignificant compared to the fire from which it emanates, but its infinite insignificance only concerns its outward form. The soul is hidden and knows nothing of its real nature, but when it awakens and begins to love again, and is filled with an inexpressible longing to return to God, it partakes of his nature, his fullness, pureness, freedom, and eternity. Then it is stripped of all selfishness and strives for nothing but giving joy to God. Then, in devoted service, it can become a part of the divine inner life."

"Is not the highest goal knowing the truth?" I asked. "My guru taught me so."

"Wisdom is not attained by wanting to know, but by devoted service alone. Wanting to know is still selfishness and a desire to satisfy egoism."

"Is not shanti, divine peace, the highest?" I asked. "Think of the Buddhist sculptures. Think of the inexpressible peace in the calm smile of the meditating Buddha's countenance. Are not all the religions of the world united in their prayer for the blessing of peace? 'May the Lord bless thee and preserve thee; may he turn his countenance to thee and give thee peace.'"

"Yes, religions are united in praying for peace, since they are still in a preparatory state and are like lessons for obstinate children. They think the only important thing is the washing away of the filth of the earth and the world's struggle. Observe the various religious devotees," continued Sadananda distressedly. "All of them want something of God, as if God were a shopkeeper. One demands power. Another prays for victory for his side and miserable defeat for the opponent. The Christian asks to enter heaven and enjoy eternal blessedness there. The Hindu wishes to be freed from Samsara, the burning wheel of the world of change, and then safely sink into rapture for eternity. The Buddhist wishes to enter Nirvana. All want the same thing, an assurance of peace, security, freedom from suffering. The case is the same with the followers of Shankaracharya. They want to become a part of Brahman and sink into the formless divine light, where all dissension vanishes. Or they even desire to become like God. You, too, Walther Eidlitz, are among these. Did you not sing as you wandered in Himalaya, 'Aham brahmasmi...I am Brahman'? Moreover, you have thoroughly misunderstood this sentence from the Upanishads. It means: In my innermost soul I am of the nature of Brahman, just as the spark is of the same nature as fire."

Sadananda stopped speaking. In silence we walked up and down the length of the barbed-wire fence. Around the camp the jackals were shrieking, gradually withdrawing deeper into the forest.

"Shri never insisted that peace was the highest aim," I resumed after a while. "Rather, he said, 'For the time being, I shall grant you only peace.' And I did not even succeed in attaining peace."

Sadananda laid his hand gently on my shoulder. "Do not grieve, Vamandas, because you are crushed and believe you have lost everything. Krishna is sometimes called Anathabandhu, the Friend of the Lordless, the lord over those who no longer own anything but their destitution and their longing for him. Believe me,

Krishna rejoices more over one who longs to love and serve him even in the crowds and the dirt of the barracks within this barbed wire, than over one who meditates in the quiet of a clean, calm forest, or a room behind padded doors. You belong to Krishna. And your meditation, your success and failure, and even your illnesses are his. But whoever dares completely to subject himself to God on his terms instead of his own? Many have tried to follow the example of a divine savior, and say like him: 'Thy will be done, not mine.' But when matters become serious, when the will of God overcomes one, fear creeps in and one whispers in secret: 'No, I meant not thus—so far, but no further.' No one wants to believe that God can make his appearance in the form of a catastrophe, a complete breakdown. But believe me, if one can prevail upon oneself in the hands of God, he need never worry. God takes over the responsibility for him, for all his actions. Then it is of no consequence whether he happens to be in an abyss in the world of change or in the kingdom of heaven, for he is always in God's kingdom of love, playing a part in the drama of God and his eternal followers, of which the world knows nothing.

"Peace, *nirvana*, longed for by so many, is only an intermediary state on the path to God's real kingdom. To be sure, many remain forever in this wonderful anteroom. But he who dares to penetrate farther, with a desire to devote himself to God yet more, does not lose peace thereby. True peace is not just freedom from stress. The freedom from passion, so highly valued by the Indian yogi, is very much overestimated. True peace means preserving the certainty that in the depth of one's being one is inseparably united with God, in all situations and through all suffering."

We walked silently for a while. "Swamiji," I asked quietly, "what has your guru told you about his understanding of why we live? Why do we have these earthly bodies?"

Sadananda became ardent. "My guru said, 'We have been given this sluggish body to let the fire of every breath we take consume it in our devotion to God.' But I do not expect you to understand this as yet, Vamandas. You do not even know yet who God, who Krishna, is…"

"Oh, how I wish I could behold God," I said.

"It is not a question of your beholding God," my companion corrected me severely. "It is much more a question of God seeing you, that He may be drawn to you by the beauty and purity in your longing for affectionate devotion. When a person wants to see God, this wish is often a desire for self-advancement. Just as humans degrade all earthly phenomena in their selfishness, by transforming them to objects, relating them to themselves, and enjoying them, so do some of them try to enjoy God."

"How can I free myself from such egoism?" I asked.

"One should not ask such questions," answered Sadananda harshly. "Even this question arises out of egoism. Pray to Krishna, the Unknown, the Hidden, to give you the strength sometime in the future to beg to serve him truly, and learn to love him.…It is late. We must sleep. Good night, Vamandas."

CHAPTER XVII

TEACHER AND DISCIPLE

Teaching in the midst of distractions—Sadananda's story—The golden avatar—The professor of mathematics who taught Sadananda—Prisoners' oaths, and verses from the Bhagavata—Spies and questioning

This meeting on the dark football field opened the way for many similar dialogues with Sadananda. Often our conversation turned quite unexpectedly in this direction, as we wandered up and down the length of the barbed-wire fence, and often even in the daytime, when sitting in the midst of a crowd of noisy fellow prisoners, peeling potatoes outside the kitchen barrack. He could fling out a short utterance, the meaning of which was not understood by the others. Sometimes he sought me in my barrack, or I came to him and sat an hour or so on his bed. He lived very uncomfortably. His neighbor was a musician who had become degenerate in the tropics, and who most of the time smelled strongly of liquor. He traded in all kinds of wares with his bed as his headquarters and presently played an old gramophone that he had recently acquired. But Sadananda was kindly disposed toward this neighbor. He did not differentiate between people with civil virtues and the so-called asocial element. He even held that a criminal or a harlot often had greater prospects for a sudden and complete conversion than a law-abiding citizen. There were many examples of this in the holy scriptures of India, as well as in the Gospels. He referred to the stories of Maria Magdalena and the robber on the cross.

Every time I came to Sadananda during those days, a most frightful noise met my ears as I entered the door. Bartering was going on from the bed of his neighbor, and, furthermore, card players sat around the only table in the barrack, slamming down dirty cards. Often, they got into arguments with one another. Sadananda did not seem to be the least disturbed by all this. He called out cheerfully, "So nice of you to come and call on me, Vamandas. Come and sit on my bed." A bright dome of peace seemed to hover invisibly over his miserable camp bed. When he began his narration, my ears became deaf to all the noise.

"What brought you to India?" I asked him.

"The longing of my heart. And my meeting Swami Bon, an Indian who had been sent to Europe by his teacher, my guru, later on. And above all, an Indian book that I came across in the library of the University of Berlin. It was a book about Krishna Chaitanya."

"Ah, the secret avatar of the age of darkness, the golden avatar! Shri told me about him."

A smile broke out on Sadananda's severe countenance. "So Shri has told you about Krishna Chaitanya," he said gladly. "According to what you have said, I thought that your teacher belonged to the school of Shankaracharya. You know, of course, that Chaitanya entered the order of Shankaracharya to redeem it from within, since his teaching contained only a half-truth."

"Is not Shankaracharya right? Isn't the world corruptible, an illusion and a delusion, yet filled with heavy pain?"

"Yes, but at the same time the world has its foundation always in God, the eternal God full of blessedness."

"Yes, of course, what we think of as the world is really the impersonal, divine Brahman," I said.

"The impersonal Brahman is only the radiancy from the figure of the personal God…It is not as simple as you believe, Vamandas. In God, the most unbelievable opposites are harmoniously united. God is simultaneously personal and impersonal. The world is separate from God, and at the same time not separate from God. The divine savior, the avatar, is separate from God and yet not separate from him. The teaching of *bhedabheda*, of being separate yet not separate, as Krishna Chaitanya has explained it, is inexhaustible. When I investigated the different systems of the Western and Eastern philosophers during my studies, I always wished that I might come across a philosophical system in which we would continue eternally without coming to an end. I have found everything I searched for in the philosophy of Krishna Chaitanya and his disciples, the treasures of which the world has not the faintest notion."

"And your own guru?"

"My guru Bhakti-Siddhanta Sarasvati was a follower of Krishna Chaitanya, and he lived in the love of God and made it known."

With great affection and tenderness, Sadananda began to tell me about his guru. In his youth, this man had been a well-known professor of higher mathematics and astronomy at a college in Bengal. One day the young scholar went to a hermit in the forest, and asked to be initiated. The spiritual teacher he had sought was a wandering ascetic, almost naked, who wore only a loin cloth. His name was Gaura Kishora. The old man harshly ignored the wish of the scholar. "Learning and reputation in the world mean nothing before Krishna," he said abruptly. But the professor of mathematics did not cease his prayers, and finally the old man accepted him as a disciple, persuaded by his endurance and affectionate devotion.

There were remarkable resemblances in the lives of Bhakti-Siddhanta Sarasvati, who had lived near the Ganges in India, and his European disciple, whom he called Sadananda. The latter, too, had breathed the harsh air of science in his youth. At the University of Leipzig he had studied comparative religion, learning various languages such as Pali, Sanskrit, Tibetan, Chinese, and Japanese. After receiving his doctorate degree and publishing a new edition of a well-known standard work in the history of religion, an unusually promising career as a university teacher was open to him. But he gave up his plans, got rid of all his possessions, and set out for India to sit at the feet of his guru, Bhakti-Siddhanta Sarasvati.

Sadananda showed me some photographs of his teacher. I was startled at the close resemblance between Sadananda and his guru. I looked at a photograph and at my friend, and at the photograph again. It was not enough to say that they looked like brothers; it seemed rather to be the same person at an early and a later period of life. The same carriage, the same expression, the same inner strength expressed in a gesture of the hand.

When I pointed out the resemblance to Sadananda he denied it with honest modesty. Gradually, as I learned to know my friend better, I noticed that he mourned the loss of his teacher, who had died in January 1937. There seemed to have been a deep spiritual bond between this guru and his European disciple. On one occasion, when Sadananda broke his customary reservation, he told me that Bhakti-Siddhanta Sarasvati had once uttered in the presence of a large audience (and to their great surprise), "You, Sadananda, and I—we have been together through all eternity."

"Fate has made it difficult for you," I said. "Half the world lay between you and your guru. How easily it could have happened that you had never met him."

"It was bound to be so," Sadananda replied slowly. "It was bound to be so, to find out whether my heart was strong enough to overcome all the obstacles and fight its way against the current. And yet now it seems amazing that I succeeded in finding him. However, I was only allowed to serve him for a little while this time. Next time I hope it will be longer."

"You dirty dog, didn't you hear me say ace of clubs? I'll skin you alive!" shouted one of the card players, a well-known wrestler who owned a gymnastics school in southern India. He looked like a giant suckling with swollen arm muscles and treacherous eyes.

"Yes, prick up your ears, so as not to miss any of the highly interesting conversation over there," Sadananda taunted me sorrowfully, when he noticed that I could not resist listening to the quarreling of the card players. "You ask questions from a desire for sensation, just like everybody else. How well my guru understood this, when among his last words he pointed out for us seriously, 'As you withdraw from the lotus feet of Krishna, you will be overcome in the same measure by the enticing and repulsive forces of this world.'"

"Put out the light! Put out the lights!" cried the European soldiers angrily, as they went on their round, at this late hour of the night, along the fence enclosing the Indian camp. Swearing, the card players hung blankets over the windows of the barrack. Then they continued playing.

"Take a sheet of paper and a pencil," said Sadananda. "I shall dictate a Sanskrit verse for you from the *Bhagavata* that may be of help to you.

> The knot of the heart shall be cut apart,
> all doubts shall be torn away,
> and even his Karma, his deeds,
> and the inevitable consequences of his deeds,
> shall disappear when he has beheld his Atman and God.

Many questions arose within me as I walked back in the darkness to my barrack. Questions that had troubled me my whole life, now received their answer. I was irresistibly drawn to Sadananda's quarters. But it was not so easy to visit him, for at first he and I belonged to different groups within the barbed wire. He was German and I was of Jewish birth. I was spied on incessantly, observed and questioned: "Where have you been? What have you been doing during these last hours? To whom have you spoken?" And reports of all this were sent to the delegation that was considering which of us could be set free. Again and again I had to conquer attacks of fear, break the laws of the opposing parties and ignore the rules of the boycott. Again and again I had to summon the courage needed to enable us to meet. But Sadananda appreciated my efforts.

CHAPTER XVIII

A NEW ROOMMATE

Sharing a dishwashing room with Sadananda—A new roommate—
Piercing cries in the night—Sadananda's aggressive grace—The clothes
and the real man—The breaker of enchantments

After a relocation and consequent reorganization of the entire camp, Sadananda and I were placed in the same barrack. We lived in a little room by ourselves. There was even space for a third bed between our two.

This room had been the dishwashing room in a mess hall for noncommissioned officers and was not intended as living quarters. It was built as a partition of the veranda. It was as hot as an oven in there. The tropical sun beat down on the low, slanting roof and the heavy brick walls. Besides, the athletic field was right next to it. It was impossible to open the little whitewashed window shutters, or some stray ball would be sure to break the window immediately. People sat to the left and to the right of our sleeping place all day long, crowded into tight rows on the veranda, watching the football matches. With every successful or unfortunate kick of the ball, these people shrieked enthusiastically or indignantly.

Meanwhile, my friend sat on his bed with his legs crossed under him. He worked eagerly, bending low as he wrote his comprehensive work. A little metal box, placed on his knees, served as a table. Beside him stood another larger metal trunk that held his books and manuscripts. All the volumes lay in exemplary order. My friend could lay his hands immediately on any of the pages, even in the darkness. In the lid of the open trunk was a portrait of Sadananda's guru.

Shouts and whistling sounded anew from outside. Again the football bounced against our shutters. The sound of broken glass reached our ears. I could not suppress my annoyance, which was turning into hatred of my fellows. "Is it necessary to learn to love human beings, before daring to aspire to love God?" I asked. "You cannot truly love human beings without knowing God's love," Sadananda promptly replied. "All the creatures of the world are like flowers of a flowering tree. The root of the tree is God. If you water the root, all the leaves and flowers of the tree will be refreshened. Love overflows. But you must not mistake the bodies of human beings, their sensuality and their desire, for the true person, the Atman, which for a while assumes one of these strange mantles. The Atman is not a Nazi, a communist, an Englishman, a Jew, a Brahman, a prizefighter, a man, or a woman. The infinite, inherent law of every Atman is to be Krishna's eternal servant, even if it has forgotten this. You must try to concentrate your gaze on the Atman."

"Can you do so?"

"I endeavor to do so."

In our new quarters, there was one inmate who was homeless. His monk's gown was similar to Sadananda's, although it was yellow instead of orange. He was one of the few European Buddhists in the camp. Some of them were very learned and of excellent character, but unfortunately I came into contact with an outsider. He was fat and had a naturally bald, shiny head. His name was Gross.

Gross's life was strange indeed. In his youth he had stood in a shop in a little town, where he sold herrings and cheese. Later he had become a strolling photographer, snapping photographs of the visitors at various seaside resorts, masculine and feminine, in more or less stages of undress. He was seized with a longing for peace and certainty, and he made his way to Ceylon, where he became a Buddhist monk. His tangled life and aggressive nature made him unsuitable, however, for the difficult mental work demanded by the teachings of Buddha.

Outwardly, he kept the rules of this order very strictly. At roll-call, mornings and evenings, he refused to stand in line with his fellow prisoners. He would not take part in the work divided up by the others, such as peeling potatoes, chopping wood, and other duties. He explained that the rules of his order forbade his performing work for laymen. He succeeded in holding his point of view.

With slow, dignified steps, his gaze fastened on the ground, he wandered up and down the length of the barbed-wire fencing, his fat body wrapped in a yellow gown. Now and then he succeeded in finding a disciple who would walk beside him for a few days, listen to his discourse, and later on desert him and make fun of him. He was considered an intolerant spreader of slander and ugly rumors.

After the reorganization of the camp, all the barracks refused to harbor Gross. Defiantly, he placed his bed outdoors near the football field, where the yellow clothes he hung were a source of annoyance to many.

"He is an old man," said Sadananda to me. "Winter is cold here. There is room in our nook. Shall we invite Gross to live with us?"

"He is aggressive," I said cautiously. "There will be unpleasantness. I know that he has told many that I practice black magic."

"Gross hasn't the slightest idea of what black magic is, and those who listen to him have still less," laughed Sadananda. "But in any case, it is wrong of them to scoff at his monk's gown."

I do not know Sadananda's real intentions, whether he wanted to give me a picture of how one should be or how one should not be. Our new roommate moved in ceremoniously and camped between our two beds. He lent me a book in which I found a citation from Buddha I never forgot:

> 'He scorned me, he beat me,
> he conquered me by force!'
> If you make room for this thought,

you cannot be free of hate.
For through this hate,
there will be no peace upon earth.
Only by not hating can hatred find peace.

Behind his mosquito net and the yellow cloths he hung over it, Gross sat every day on his bed between Sadananda's and mine, meditating for many hours with his legs crossed. He always carried a skull with him, and, placing it before him, he meditated on the corruptibility of the earth. "I radiate sympathy and love for all human beings," he told me. But in spite of his deep trance, Gross was remarkably well aware of what was going on about him. Though he had given up all possessions, he insisted upon all his personal rights, such as his share of the floor. He was not so eager, however, when it was a question of sweeping this floor—the rules of his order forbade him. "I understand that you wish to pick a quarrel with me," he said to me several times. Both Sadananda and I walked on tiptoe so as not to disturb him.

Gross had the peculiarity of often emitting piercing cries in his sleep, calling out "huhuhu" as if he were having a nightmare.

"Don't shriek like that," said Sadananda harshly, when it became unbearable, and he turned on the light. We were in the habit of turning off the light before the required time so that our roommate might sleep undisturbed.

Gross sat up, blinking, and it took some time for him to come to his senses. "No wonder I shout in my sleep," he said deliberately. "There are two ears too many in this room." He glanced meaningfully in my direction, for he was hinting at the secret artifices which, according to his belief, I practiced in order to upset him.

At this, Sadananda dropped all his deference. He did not call our roommate "your reverence," nor did he address him by his Buddhist monk's name, as he usually did out of respect for the gown Gross wore. He called him by his old name from the days of the ware shop. "Gross, don't try anything like that," he reprimanded him. "You don't shriek because of any dark and evil things around you, but because you yourself are filled with ugly secret thoughts. That is why you are tortured by nightmares. Because of this, you live steadily in agony and believe that others threaten you. You declare that you radiate sympathy and love, but instead you nurse your hatred. You say that you practice contemplation, but instead you sit there like a spider in its web, listening for something that might disturb you, so that afterward you can complain about it. I have never in all my life seen anyone so thoroughly enveloped in egoism as you. You believe yourself to be the center of the world that surrounds you. You dishonor the respectable monk's gown of Buddha that you wear, you old hypocrite!"

With his fat countenance drawn into lines meant to express the fact that he was accustomed to suffering the bitterness of injustice, Gross listened to this torrent of words. With the same expression on his face, he moved the next day, taking his skull and his writings on mercy and love somewhere else.

"Why were you so harsh with Gross?" I asked when our roommate had left us.

"To awaken his Atman, his soul. Even if he runs away now with his feelings outraged and injured, the impression will remain until his next incarnation. This was a far better way of helping him than if I had nourished his egoism and vanity. My guru was a master in this manner of helping. He called it 'aggressive grace,' grace through attack. But in the West it is so easy to mistake the garments for the true figure. You know that I value the social endeavor of the West very highly. Yes, welfare institutions for the old and the sick, the right of all to have work and education—it is excellent, all of it. Protection for children and those who are ill, weak, or persecuted, this must exist. In our days it is, in fact, almost the only thing that distinguished humans from animals. But when I think of all these efforts at making the corruptible, changeable world pleasant for humans, it often seems to me to be as if somebody had fallen in the water and was in danger of drowning. Then another comes running to help him and manages to rescue his clothes, his hat, and his spectacles. The drowning man himself, the Atman, is allowed to go under."

Gradually, I learned that every word uttered by Sadananda was an expression of his soul, and all his actions, whether friendly or scornful—he could be exceedingly harsh and stern—were based on an effort to awaken the Atman in the people he contacted. In spite of his monk's gown, which invited derision, the inmates of the camp respected him. They were afraid of him because he was quicker than they were at repartee. He made them uneasy, and they avoided him.

When Sadananda injured someone's feelings, his words could wound deep enough to cause tears. Whoever experienced this often felt as if the very foundation of his being had been uprooted. But the painful blow did not come from the intolerant sword of violence. It was more like a purifying flash of lightning. It was the same kind of blow with which many of our fairy tales end. There the enchanted person begs, "Cut off my head. Cut off the animal head that has been placed on me." If the other hesitates, the enchantment is not broken. But if the rescuer strikes, the enchanted person is freed from the curse and assumes their true form again.

But it is only in fairy tales that enchanted beings have the courage to say, "Break the enchantment, give me the true shape of love. Strike, delivering sword!" In the camp they spoke unkindly of Sadananda. "He is a renegade who has betrayed his European birth and become a nigger." Hateful reports and false accusations were sent to the investigation committee.

CHAPTER XIX

THE CHURCH BEHIND THE BARBED WIRE

The imprisoned missionaries—Old Pater Lader—Dr. Fuchs, the Protestant priest—Jesuits with notebooks—Sadananda's lectures— Theological controversies—The guru holds his own

There were a great many Christian missionaries confined in the camp, in nearly every section. The entire life of the church and all its difficulties were revealed within the barbed-wire enclosure. In the intimacy of life in the barracks, it became apparent that mortals were hidden inside clergyman's apparel, with the usual human weaknesses. Still, it was often a great comfort to know that within the camp, which was rife with hate and quarreling, some people endeavored to fix their gaze on eternal matters.

For example, every Catholic priest in the camp held a quiet service each morning, and on Sundays an altar was raised in the dining-room barrack. I rejoiced when on Easter Day this room shook with jubilation over the Resurrection, and when Catholics and Protestants together joined in the choir singing. I tried honestly to see the priests of the various faiths as successors to Christ's followers, to whom he once said, "Receive the Holy Spirit! Go out for my sake, and make all people your disciples, baptizing them in the name of the Father, the Son, and the Holy Ghost."

But bearing the message of the Holy Ghost out into the world also means acknowledging the Holy Ghost in all his manifestations. I had learned to know the love of God, as Sadananda explained it, as a revelation which glowed with a holy spirit. I was very surprised by the fact that many "Christians" spoke with contempt of Sadananda. It also surprised me that most of them had not the slightest conception of India's ancient stream of pure theism. The priests and other spiritual brethren spoke condescendingly of the "poor heathens," among whom Sadananda was included. Only one of the many Christian missionaries I met in the prison camp had acquainted himself with the culture and religion of the people they had set out to convert. Many of them, however, tried to make up for their neglect in this matter during their imprisonment.

It was a strange little group that gathered regularly in our washroom, over the noise of football enthusiasts and big leather balls hitting our wall.

I remember some of those who attended Sadananda's course very well. Old Pater Lader sat there on a stool that he had brought along. His rough workman's hands were clasped on his knees. His coarse, wrinkled face was surrounded by an unkempt grayish beard. His fellow-clergymen laughed at "Kind Pater Lader," for he was not very particular about his appearance, and his white monk's cowl was often stained or fastened wrong. In his youth he had been a blacksmith's journeyman in Württemburg. Called by some inner urge, he had joined a religious order and traveled to India—only to be put into an Indian prison camp for six years during the First World War. Between the two wars he had studied Latin, worked his way through a seminary and had been ordained as a priest. After that, he had lived for many years in an Indian village in the midst of the jungle, in solitude, poverty, and the greatest privation.

"You don't know the Indian village," he had said to me. "You know nothing about the superstition and fanaticism in such a village. Your are acquainted only with the highest Indian culture and the Upanishads."

And yet he loved that Indian village, although he had seldom succeeded in converting anyone during his long years of service. He loved the Upanishads, too. In the early days of my imprisonment he had come to me to borrow some Sanskrit texts. Of the many Christian missionaries I got to know in the camp, old Lader was the only one who had learned Sanskrit before entering the camp.

Beside Lader sat a Protestant priest, Dr. Fuchs. He wore well-fitting, spotless clothes, smiled complacently most of the time, and had a private like for intrigue. But he was a talented man and had a longing in his soul. He often came to us in the little washroom, even when no lectures were in progress. Sadananda was harsh with him, as he was with all those of whom he expected anything. "He could have great possibilities," Sadananda said of him. "But he has had too much external success. He needs a hard blow of destiny that could crush him completely. Then his soul could really awaken."

Beside Pastor Fuchs sat a layman, a quiet, white-haired geologist. Before his imprisonment, Dr. Schultheiss had explored mines in South America and India. So far he had only dealt with purely natural science and had been a convinced atheist. After one of Sadananda's lectures he said to me seriously, "Whoever could have believed that anything like this was possible? The world in which I have lived is not the complete world. It is as if a veil has been drawn aside. I feel a breeze from another, truer reality when your friend speaks of Krishna." He looked at me aghast. "Have we entirely forgotten the real world?"

Dr. Schultheiss' wife was imprisoned a thousand miles away in the women's camp in south India, where I had stayed a short while. After many years, the married couples were finally reunited in a newly erected, barbed-wire-enclosed family prison camp, and Dr. Schultheiss left us. He wrote to Sadananda many times, and sent him as a Christmas gift a carved wooden plate that he had made.

Three Jesuits tirelessly noted Sadananda's words in memorandum books they held on their knees. They were used to studying for examinations, and were also acquainted with scientific work. Not until they are forty-five years of age are they full-fledged members of their order. The novices wasted no time in the camp; they listened to lectures as previously. The Jesuits had established a complete theological faculty in the prison camp. The three who attended Sadananda's course were as unlike one another as they could be.

Young Pater Zehner did not make much of a stir. Nobody in the camp spoke unkindly of him, in spite of his white cowl and the beard that framed the furrowed brown face from which his large eyes looked out. Without being asked, he went ahead and helped when a heavy trough of potatoes had to be carried to the kitchen, or when volunteers were sought for some difficult task. It was pleasant to sit beside him when sharing work with him. When he spoke, he chose his words carefully. "We too have them," he mumbled approvingly, when Sadananda hinted at the secrets of the divine inner life mirrored in the cult of Radha-Krishna. Zehner spoke of the love that flows between the three divine persons of the Trinity, but he was evidently quite embarrassed at his own words.

Sonnenbichler was as strong as a lion and looked like the archangel Michael carved in wood. At that time he was still only a novice, but one of the interned Italian bishops came over to ordain him. The tall, light-haired youth lay prone during the service like the trunk of a fallen tree before the altar in the dining-room barrack. For days after the ceremony, he went about in a trance. In reality his wish had been to become a sculptor. "Oh, how terribly difficult it is to learn Sanskrit," he groaned, as we rinsed our tin plates one day. "How much easier Latin is! And those new, subtle lines of thought, that mobile thinking that one must master first…My brain refuses. It rises like an unruly horse."

"It was exactly the same for me in the beginning," I comforted him.

Like Sonnenbichler, Pater Sprechmann, the third Jesuit attending Sadananda's course, came from a village in Bavaria. His accent betrayed him, even though his theological studies at the University of Freiburg had put a veil of scholasticism over his country-bred straightforwardness. His eager, forced speech often hurried far ahead of his thoughts. It sometimes seemed as if he wanted to seize the divine secrets with a crowbar. Dr. Sprechmann was versatile and ambitious. He was not only a theologian, but also an excellent athlete and long-distance runner, and he trained daily in the gymnastic hall. One of his aims was to win the "gold medal" for athletics in the camp.

Sadananda stood before the borrowed blackboard dressed in an orange-colored garment, wearing common Indian sandals. "The Krishna you have heard about, the divine hero and teacher in the epic *Mahabharata* and in the *Bhagavad-gita,* is not the complete Krishna," he explained. "Even the divinity who is the foundation of the world, the God who creates, holds, and maintains the world, receiving it at last into himself—these are only outer aspects of Krishna. The true Krishna is a deep mystery."

Sadananda wrote on the blackboard in his fine, bold handwriting the syllable *Krish* in the Devanagari script.

"The word *Krishna* comes from the Sanskrit root *Krish*, which means 'to attract,' " he explained. "There is not only physical gravitation, but spiritual as well. Just as the physical sun attracts the earth and the planets so that they rotate about it, so does Krishna attract the souls, the Atmas of all beings, to himself by means of love and indescribable beauty. Krishna is throughout consciousness. He is described as 'the spiritual sun of all consciousness.' The human soul stands in the same relation to him, to God, as the rays of the sun to the sun itself."

Sadananda searched among his papers. "I shall dictate a hymn to Krishna from the Middle Ages. It originates from Jagadananda, a devoted friend and disciple of Chaitanya:

> Man is a mortal speck of spiritual consciousness; Krishna is the sun of all that is spiritually conscious. Those who behold Krishna eternally, love and honor him. He who turns away his face from Krishna, makes place for desire. Maya, who is near him, seizes and embraces him. When the demon assumes the upper hand, the spirit is destroyed.

The same thing happens when Man falls into Maya's clutches. "I am the servant of Krishna," this he had forgotten. He becomes a wage earner of Maya and wanders about aimlessly, sometimes a demigod, sometimes a demon, sometimes master, sometimes slave...

By those dedicated to God, he learns the truth about his own being. When he knows this, he no longer bothers about the changeable world. Weeping, he cries: "Oh, Krishna, I am after all thy servant. When I left thy feet, I reaped only destruction." And if only once he calls in prayer "Krishna!" Krishna is merciful and frees him from the changeable world. He leaves Maya behind him, and yearns to serve Krishna. And lovingly, lovingly he approaches the lotus feet of Krishna.

"But what is Maya?" asked Sprechmann. "One often hears the word Maya, and now you use it. I find it interesting. Will you explain its meaning?"

"Gladly," answered Sadananda. "The infinite power of God appears in two aspects, attractive and repulsive, leading to the feet of God, and driving away from the feet of God. Think of the two forces centripetal and centrifugal. The force which, according to God's will, drives away from him and hides him, is Maya."

"I do not understand what you mean by 'the force that, according to God's will, drives one away from him and hides him,'" muttered Dr. Sprechmann.

Sadananda wrote on the blackboard the syllable *ma*. "The word *maya* comes from the Sanskrit root *ma*," he explained calmly. But a secret fire, familiar to me, flashed in his eyes. "*Ma* means to measure. As long as we egotistically measure the things about us, value them according to the measure of joy or pain they give us, we are in the power of Maya, who hides God from us. By God's decree, she rules the measurable universe."

"Does not the universe belong to God?" I asked.

"Maya's universe exists, by God's grace, for souls who do not serve and love him, but rather wish to enjoy egotistically."

"The universe is therefore a concentration camp of God?" Dr. Schultheiss shot in, dismayed.

"No, an educational institution," my friend replied calmly. "When we notice that suffering and bitterness lie at the bottom of every pleasure, and when we turn again toward God, we touch his heart and he draws us back to him. But we cannot conceive of such a thing with our senses and our measuring intelligence. As long as we degrade the phenomena of the world by making them objects of our desire for pleasure, we can understand neither the world nor God. God's real existence is absolutely inapproachable for our logic."

Sprechmann raised his forefinger. "Do you deny therefore the possibility of logical evidence of God? If so, I must oppose this."

Pastor Fuchs cleared his throat. "For once I have the same opinion as the Catholic Church."

"The Mother Church," said Pater Lader slowly.

"Is not our universe, with its innumerable Milky Ways, that lie millions and billions of light years away—is not every drop of water a testimony of the majesty of God?" continued Dr. Fuchs, now in a loud unctuous voice. "My point of view is, the further we penetrate the secrets of the universe with modern natural science, the nearer we approach God."

"The brain of man can probably imagine a faint shadow of that aspect of God which is turned toward the world," said Sadananda. "But God does not exist only in his majestic aspect. God does not exist only for the sake of the world. Even a few European mystics acknowledge this. God has a personal existence. Our universe, bound by time and space, has the same relation to God's kingdom as the barracks on the seashore have to the boundless sea. I can only repeat that one cannot enter God's kingdom by wanting to know, but only through loving devotion."

"You spoke earlier about the force that draws us to the feet of God," said Pater Zehner slowly. "Did you not call that force Radha?"

Sadananda's pale face brightened. Silence filled the room for a moment. "Radha is a personification, the original shape of the love of God. No one can approach God without the permission of Radha, without her bearing one's soul."

Sadananda wrote the syllable *radh* on the blackboard. "The word *Radha* comes from *radh*," he said. "The Sanskrit root *radh* means *reverent love*. Affectionate reverence is not measurable, for even if love increases for all eternity, it yet has no end, no bottom. And the immeasurable kingdom of God is woven of love."

Pater Zehner nodded happily.

Sadananda continued. "In the hidden kingdom of God, Radha serves Krishna with indescribable loving devotion. At the same time, She is one with him in the same way as the glow of the fire is of the fire, and as the scent of the rose is one with the rose. Radha never leaves the innermost kingdom of God. But one of her aspects is mercifully turned towards the world. In Christian theology, that aspect is called the Holy Ghost."

The fountain pens of the Jesuits glided quickly over the paper.

"I believe you have heard enough for today," said Sadananda, and closed his volume. Those attending the lecture left us.

Sadananda bent down over the open trunk containing his books and carefully laid in the papers he had used. Silently, he looked at the picture of his guru.

"I know, of course, that my efforts will not bear fruit this time," he said. "I am probably giving one or two of my listeners material that can later on be used in controversial treatises against Indian theism. But in any case, I force them to pronounce the name Krishna, to listen to the name Krishna. And I am convinced that the divine name Krishna has so much power that it can help them approach the inner kingdom of God in their next incarnation."

CHAPTER XX

THE NAME OF GOD

We travel a thousand miles—The name of God—Mystical power of sound—Importance of the names of God—Meditation on the logos—Monkeys race after our train

One day I happened to hear the mantra of the name of God on Sadananda's lips. It was on an occasion when the whole camp had again moved, more than a thousand miles away, from the barbed-wire enclosure in south India to newly erected ones in north India at the foot of Himalaya. We had been on our way several days and still had much of the journey ahead of us. All of us were locked into railway carriages with all our belongings, and we were carefully guarded. Sadananda was leaning out of an open window in an old, third-class carriage for Indian soldiers and seemed oblivious to those around him. He sang out into the wind just as the sun sank behind the golden Indian plains.

The words were familiar to me; the melody, too. Where had I heard them before? My heart vibrated longingly at the sound, like a tuning fork awakened by harmonizing tones.

It was the same wonderful sound that had met my ears one evening shortly after my arrival in India. Shri and I had ascended a flight of weathered steps in the midst of Himalaya's flowering forests, and we were greeted by the song of the monks from the terrace of the pilgrim shelter. The sound, and the secret I suspected behind it, had attracted me irresistibly, stronger than anything I had ever experienced. I had pursued the sound, seeking it in vain—and now I had found it on a prisoner's train that was rolling through India.

133

Night had fallen. The good-natured Indian soldiers who guarded us leaned forward wearily as they sat with loaded guns between their knees. My comrades were playing cards. "What was that you sang just now?" I asked.

Sadananda looked at me questioningly, as if seeing deep down into my soul. "That was the mantra of the name of God," he said.

Outside the train windows it was getting darker.

"Sound is the first revelation of the divine world in which the soul can participate," he said. "Before beholding the kingdom of God, one hears it with an inner ear. Think of Logos, the word of God, from which all things have come to be. But the words of all languages—even Sanskrit—are of an earthly nature, with one exception: the name of God. More precisely, the names of God. For in his mercy, God has revealed to us many of his names, both outer and inner, which encompass the whole of his divine power.

"The *Padma Purana* says, 'The name of God is spiritual substance, pure, eternal, and perfectly free from matter, since God's name is not separate from God.' The name of God, therefore, can not only wash away all sins, but it can even untie the knot of the heart and awaken the love of God.

"When one whose Atman is completely awakened sings the name of God, this has the power of waking a sleeping soul. What happens then is called initiation."

The song of the wheels sounded monotonously against the rails.

"And meditation, yoga...all the other paths to God, which Shri spoke of and which the *Bhagavad-gita* mentions, and the Gospels...?

"There are many paths. But we Bhaktas are convinced that the present age, Kaliyuga, has shrouded these paths in darkness. When one sings the name of God, however, the darkness is dispelled. Krishna Chaitanya, the golden avatar of Kaliyuga, has brought the name of God to earth as no other Savior before him has done. Hundreds of times he repeated that for the name of God, except for the name of God, verily, except for the name of God, there is nowhere, nowhere, nowhere, a refuge in our dark age.

"Of course," continued Sadananda, "you must not believe that anyone who mentions the word *Krishna,* utters the name of God. The earthly clang of the name, which your physical ears can detect, is only a vessel for the spiritual clang, or the shadow of the spiritual clang. It has been said, 'Krishna's name, and all that is contained in that name, cannot be perceived by the physical senses. But when a person turns to Krishna with a desire to serve him, the name reveals itself to his tongue.' But even the shadow of God's name is capable of doing a great deal. It helps lead the heart toward God. It washes away sin. Do you know what sin is, Vamandas? To be severed from God is the only real sin."

The lights of Delhi were getting nearer, as were the endless rows of houses, homes for clerks, coolies, and street sweepers, civil service men and workers in the capital city of India. In a brightly lit parlor car that slowly glided along toward the big city on a side-track, two persons were seated. One was a high English government official dressed in a dinner suit, probably the governor of one of the provinces, corpulent and decrepit, yet forceful in appearance like an ancient Roman procurator. And in the easy chair opposite sat his elderly spouse in evening gown, highly rouged and rigid. These two people, in sorry loneliness, seemed to be the only passengers in the elegant railway carriage.

Our train went on; the big city was already behind us. Sadananda slept soundly on the seat beside mine, hardly an arm's length away. Our comrades slept on the wooden berths, one over another. Only the guards sat up, their guns between their knees. The window opened out to the moonlit night. I looked out at the unfamiliar landscape and saw swaying palm tops, well sweeps, cranes, and storks. Great wild peacocks, Krishna's sacred animals, danced in the moonlight.

The name of God…I was thinking. Strange and unfamiliar were the things that my friend had just confided to me. And yet the Indian night seemed to me only a thin, fluttering veil behind which the secret was being carried toward my heart.

The *name* of God, which awakens love…"I have proclaimed them thy *name*, and shall proclaim it, that the love thou hast given me may be theirs, and I myself may be theirs." These words of Christ to God, Christ's last, most sacred words in the circle of his disciples after Communion, came to me out of the blue Indian night.

"Our father, which art in heaven, hallowed be thy *name*." Christ's words to his divine father when the disciples stood on the mountain beside him and asked, "How shall we pray?" sounded in my ears.

"I baptize you in the *name* of the Father, and of the Son, and of the Holy Ghost, amen." The ancient formula for baptizing echoed about me.

"Where two or three are gathered in my *name*, there am I also." I was moved as never before by the words of the Savior.

I recalled, too, a day long ago on the island of Patmos in the Aegean Sea. In the library of the cloister, a Greek Orthodox priest opened for me and my wife the stiff, enormous pages of a manuscript of a Gospel from the ancient Christian era. It was written with silver letters on purple parchment, but the names of God and Christ shone brighter than the rest of the writing. They were written in letters of gleaming gold.

Had we forgotten the loving power of the name of God? Was it necessary to travel to India to rediscover the secret?

Logos, the word of God, sounded through the Indian holy writings and the words of joy with which Krishna Chaitanya, the hidden avatar of the Dark Age, has praised the power of the name of God:

> The name of God cleanses the mirror of the human heart.
> It quenches the great forest fire of suffering
> from the cycle of births and deaths.
> It is like moonlight that opens
> the lotus chalice of goodness in the human heart.

The name of God is the inner life of beloved Lady Wisdom.
It lets the ocean of divine bliss increase ever more.
It gives the taste of divine abundance
at every syllable of the holy name.
The name of God bathes the whole soul.

The night was heavy with the scent of flowers. The pleasant odor of the flowering mango trees floated in to the sleepers on the northbound train. It seemed as if I were being transported on a boat out onto a boundless sea of divine love, whose waves enveloped each coastline, each earthly horizon. The waves rose higher and higher.

Dawn came. Sadananda half-reclined on his seat and gazed out of the open window. I touched his hand. "Initiate me in the name of God," I implored.

Once again my friend looked at me as though he were searching my soul. "I am not a guru," he said. "My task in this life is to lead people to the feet of my guru. I hope you will find your guru, and that he will receive you."

The train thundered over an iron bridge. Down in the depths, the silver-gray water of a river glittered in the light of dawn. "The Ganges," said Sadananda. "Not far from here, at Rishikesh. It breaks through the mountain chain of Himalaya."

Once more I had reached Kailas, the home of Shiva.

Our train stopped at a station. "Hardvar," I read.

"One of India's seven ancient holy cities," my friend informed me. "For that matter, you have studied Sanskrit. What does Hardvar mean?"

"Of course I know. Hari-dvara means the portal of Hari, the portal of God."

Below the railway we could see cupolas and the flat white roof of a temple. Great flocks of monkeys played undisturbed on its roof. They were considered followers of Hanuman, chief of the monkeys, initiated by God.

As if by command, the monkeys swung from the roof and the walls and ran after the long train, which had been set in motion again. It slowly puffed its way up the steep incline through the forest.

Delighted at the unexpected diversion, the prisoners leaned out of the windows, shrieking taunting invectives at the monkeys, and threw down whatever they could find in the way of empty cigar and cigarette boxes, metal objects, and tin cans, until the apes gave up the chase and turned back.

"I have lain thinking all night about the name of God," I said.

Sadananda nodded gladly. "Yes, I know. He who has once been overwhelmed by the magnetic power of God, by the jubilant rejoicing power of God, can never escape it."

CHAPTER XXI

HUMAN GOALS

The new prison camp—Reading the Bhagavata in a toolshed—The tale of King Parikshit—Overthrow of Kali, the Dark One—Meeting with an aged Brahman hermit—Cursed by the Brahman's son—Belated regrets—The holy Shuka—The dying king attains the goal of life— What is the highest goal?—Love greater than liberation

The mountains were green and wet with rain, but all the beauty of the Indian landscape seemed to fade as we entered the double barbed-wire entrance of the new camp, dragging our baggage with us. The tangle of rusty barbed wire was like that of all the other camps we had occupied, and the people there were also the same as before. They had brought along all their passions, their griefs, and their fates. It was not long before the grass in the crowded square was trampled and the earth robbed of its luster. But the light within me had not been extinguished. It streamed forth from my heart, hung on the name of God which Sadananda had sung during our journey.

In the new camp, Sadananda and I were no longer together in the same barrack. Sadananda had been directed to the southern section, where the Buddhist monks lived. I had the good fortune to live alone for a while in a toolhouse in the northern section, near the barbed-wire fence. This was a friendly gesture on the part of the commander of the camp, and I was very envied.

However, the four large window openings directly under the roof had no glass, and the door was cracked. The birds flew as they pleased through the open spaces between the roof and the wall.

Right beside the toolshed stood the canteen common to all who lived in this section of the camp, where home-brewed ale and liquor were served until late at night, which naturally did not take place noiselessly. But in spite of all these inconveniences, this proved to be a very happy time for me, for I could work.

My friend eagerly helped me furnish my new retreat. We found a damaged tabletop in a heap of rubbish, and somewhere else, two iron supports on which to place it. These had been deemed too unsteady for use in the dining room, but they were good enough for us. We spread a blue linen cloth on the table, and it really looked splendid. Sadananda, who was very handy, stood on a stool that we had placed on the rickety table. As I held on to the swaying scaffolding, he nailed old sheets that I had folded and sewn together over the wide openings in the north wall, to prevent the winter winds from the mountains from blowing in.

Quite satisfied with our efforts, we sat on opposite sides of the table in the bare room. Sadananda imparted his teachings to me tirelessly, although even at that time he had begun to suffer great physical pain. He burned his candle at both ends, put his whole heart into his work, and at the same time tried to teach me spiritual devotion as he had learned it from his guru.

Sadananda and I began once more reading together there in the toolshed. We read from the old Indian work called *Bhagavata* in twelve volumes, with which I had already become acquainted at Shri's home. With Sadananda's help I read again, in the original language, the numerous stories related by the youth Shuka to King Parikshit, as the latter sat on the shore of the Ganges awaiting death.

"If I should be placed on an uninhabited island and be allowed the possession of only one book, I would surely choose the *Bhagavata* of all the books on earth," my friend remarked enthusiastically.

"Not the *Bhagavad-gita?*"

"The *Bhagavad-gita,* in spite of its greatness, is only a beginner's book. Where the *Bhagavad-gita* finishes, the secrets of the *Bhagavata* begin.

"The path on which you have set out, Vamandas, is a long one. But do not tire! How often my guru lamented the fact that he had never met anyone who was prepared to devote all his strength to translating and expounding the *Bhagavata*. I have begun, and have spent many years doing this. But my strength is not equal to the task. Will you help me? Begin by outlining the tale of King Parikshit, for his fight for righteousness and justice is probably the easiest part for a Westerner to understand."

I sat in my shed and thought, the Sanskrit word *Parikshit* means "he who has withstood the test."

Parikshit's grandfather was the famous hero Arjuna, for whom his charioteer and friend Krishna revealed the divine song called *Bhagavad-gita*.

When King Parikshit grew up, Krishna had already left the earth. The darkness of Kaliyuga had enveloped the world. Parikshit did everything in his power to re-establish the justice that had been defiled on earth. He rode through all lands in his golden fighting chariot to help humans reach the three goals set by the Vedas for each life on earth: justice, prosperity, lust for all.

I laid aside the book. This was a story highly appropriate to our own times, I thought. King Parikshit wished to make the three human goals—Dharma, Artha, Kama: justice, prosperity, lust—accessible to all beings on earth. These are the same goals that are eagerly sought by most people today. And how far has humanity come in its efforts to reach these goals? I shuddered at the thought.

I took up the *Bhagavata* again and began reading and translating anew. I had to find out how the story of King Parikshit, the tested one, developed.

Strange things followed. The king, who wished to re-establish true justice everywhere on earth, arrived at the shore of a river called Sarasvati, the river of wisdom. And here the monarch must have sunk into meditative mood. What follows must be read with eyes that see deeper than the physical surface of things. This took place in another world, a world to which our world is closely related, and which casts its great shadows over ours.

Parikshit met a figure on the shore of the river who bore the name Kali, "the Dark One." He was the ruler of Kaliyuga, the dark age of dissension in which we live today. Disguised as a monarch, Kali trampled justice everywhere.

In this vision, the earth did not resemble the planet as we know it. It appeared in the form of a cow that tearfully begged Parikshit for help. Justice appeared in the form of a white bull, which Kali beat madly with an iron staff. The wicked man had already succeeded in paralyzing three of the bull's legs. The first leg of justice was the power of the judge to see clearly in meditation; the Dark One had already paralyzed this leg completely. The second and third feet of the bull of justice were the purity of heart and mercy of the judge. These legs, too, had been paralyzed by Kali. The bull tried to hold himself up on the one leg left: truth. An arduous search for truth still exists among us, even in the dark age.

Parikshit drew his bow and approached the terrible being. Kali cast off the unseemly ruler's mantle, for he was no real king. He was cowardly and ill at ease, a low-minded shudra. He begged for mercy as he writhed on the ground, clasping the feet of Parikshit. "Wherever I flee, I shall always see thy flashing over me," he groaned. "Oh, grant me, like all others, a refuge."

"Even you shall not plead in vain for my protection," answered Parikshit. "In gambling houses, in brothels, in slaughter houses, in taverns, and in the hearts of all greedy men, you may dwell. These may be your five asylums."

Parikshit was convinced that he had bound the Dark One in an abyss from which he could not escape, but he was mistaken. Kali cast his shadow over all the earth, even into the heart of the king.

Shortly after his apparent victory over the Dark Age, King Parikshit was out one day hunting. It would have been a serious crime for a Brahman to hunt animals, but according to the rules of the warrior caste, hunting was permitted and considered chivalrous. The king had followed game a long time, and he was tired and thirsty. In vain, he sought a spring or a stream in the hot, dry forest of briars. Not a drop of water was to be found. Tortured by thirst, he came upon the twig hut of a hermit and entered it in the hope of finding something to drink.

There in the dusk sat an old man with his legs crossed, his back rigid, his eyes half-closed, deeply lost in meditation, hardly breathing.

Parikshit, whose tongue was dry and cracked with thirst, begged him, "Give me something to drink."

The old man did not answer. He did not even invite the king to sit. He did not ask him to bathe his tired, dusty feet. He did not offer him anything to drink. By doing so, he broke all the rules of hospitality that King Parikshit had established on earth. An ugly thought crept into the king's heart: "Perhaps the old man was only pretending to be lost in meditation, because he considers himself superior to me. Maybe he, a Brahman, does not wish to wait on one of the warrior caste." A wild anger that he had never known rose within him. As he turned to go, he happened to see a dead snake lying on the floor. He took up the creature with the point of his bow and threw it disdainfully about the neck of the old man. The latter did not move a muscle. King Parikshit left the hut with heavy steps.

The young son of the Brahman, a proud, beautiful boy, was playing with some other children nearby when this happened. When the boy observed the infamy inflicted on his father, he was distressed at the fact that a man of warrior caste would disrespect a Brahman. Wildly excited, he shouted to his playmates: "Oh, what injustice prevails among the rulers of the earth in this Dark Age! Since almighty Krishna is no longer here to punish the offender, I shall do so myself. You shall see!"

In his wrath, the boy cursed King Parikshit: "Seven days from now, the prince of snakes shall by my command kill the man who has broken the law and dishonored my father." Then he ran home, and when he saw that his father still sat with the dead snake hanging about his neck, he wept loudly.

The wise man heard his son's weeping and gently removed the dead body. "Why are you weeping?" he asked. The boy related what had happened. "My child, my child, what have you done!" wailed the father. "Oh, my child, you have committed a great crime without knowing it. You have invoked a severe punishment for a slight mistake. This noble king was suffering from hunger, thirst, and exhaustion. And you have dared to judge the monarch who, according to the will of God, preserves justice on earth. Oh, may almighty and ever-present God forgive you for the sin, which in your ignorance you have committed against one dedicated to God!"

Parikshit, meanwhile, regretted his actions. "Oh, how stupidly I behaved towards the holy man. Something terrible will surely happen to me, and may that punishment be prompt and severe, in order to wipe away my sin."

As he pondered this, he heard about the curse of the Brahman's son. Without hesitation, Parikshit handed over the throne to his son. He surrendered all his treasure and his flourishing, well-ordered kingdom. He left his beautiful wife. He denied all worldly things, and made a promise to fast the last seven days of his life. Everything that previously had seemed to be of importance—justice, prosperity, and lust—now appeared to be a heap of ashes. Parikshit no longer thought about earthly laws, but about things far above laws. He sat on the shore of the River Ganges and began to meditate.

Just then a group of holy men and their disciples came down to the river. Parikshit bowed low before them. He hailed each of them in turn. And when all of them had seated themselves, he stood before them with his hands clasped. "Ye wise men, help me to spend the last days of my life worthily. Teach me what he shall do who stands at death's door!"

Just then, young Shuka, son of the great Vyasa, came smilingly on his way. He wandered over the earth without desire. No caste mark could be seen on him, nor did he bear the costume of a monk or a penitent; he was naked. The vault of heaven was his only garment. He was surrounded by a swarm of children. He looked like a youth of sixteen, but the holy men recognized his radiance, and they rose respectfully.

Parikshit bowed low before the newcomer and invited him to sit down. Then the king threw himself on the ground before Shuka, who was resplendent among the holy men as the moon is among the stars, and asked Shuka to answer his question: "What shall a person do, who is standing at death's door? What shall he listen to? What shall he bear in mind? Whom shall he adore? What shall he meditate upon?"

"You have asked the most important question," said Shuka. "Your question will be of credit to the whole world. He who knows nothing of the Atman asks a thousand questions, and strives to know a thousand different things. And meanwhile, life is going by at night during sleep and in the daytime during the strife for corruptible things. But your question is loved by those who know the Atman. It speaks of the final goal."

Then Shuka began to instruct the king about the indestructible innermost being within humans, the Atman. He taught him the Atman's true foundation, God. He led the listener to Mahavishnu, in and out of whose pores float the universes, like dust specks through an open window. When Mahavishnu exhales, worlds are created; when he inhales, they are destroyed. But there will never be an end to the birth and destruction of these worlds, for Mahavishnu never ceases to breathe.

Shuka led his listener still further, through the ocean of primordial cause and the light of consciousness, into God's inner realm. Shuka spoke to the dying Parikshit of Krishna, who dwells in his own kingdom and simultaneously appears throughout the universe.

"Hunger plagues me no longer, although it has been a long time since I've eaten," said Parikshit. "I feel no thirst any longer, although I have ceased drinking water. I desire nothing other than to hear more and more about Krishna. Every word about Krishna that you speak is like nectar to me."

After seven days, Shuka went on his way. He walked along naked, dancing and singing the praise of Krishna. Children ran after him. The mermaids who played in the river were not embarrassed in the presence of the naked man. In his holy innocence, Shuka did not differentiate between man and woman. He saw only the eternal soul, the Atman in all beings. In each living thing he perceived the devoted love of the Atman for God: in flowering trees, in bushes, in humans, in animals, in rivers and mermaids, and in bright devas and demons. He saw the Atman of every being exult in the praise of God, some openly, others as yet deeply veiled. He sang as he walked.

Parikshit sat smiling and listening on the shore of the Ganges. When the poisonous snake came and bit him to death, so that in a moment his body was burnt to ashes, Parikshit did not notice, for he was already in the kingdom of God. He had not asked for release from the curse, had not prayed to be allowed to live, although Shuka could easily have freed him from the curse. He only prayed to hear more about God. Thus the curse of the Brahman's son came to be an infinite blessing for him. Because of the curse, Krishna bestowed upon him divine love, the most priceless treasure.

The next day Sadananda appeared unexpectedly in my room. He did not like to make appointments, and even in the prison camp he was as free as a bird. "Well, Vamandas," he called. "It looks as if you have been working. Have you thought about the goals of human beings?"

"Oh, yes, I have. The true human goals are not Dharma, Artha, Kama—justice, prosperity, lust—but liberation from the eternal circle of births and deaths. Mukti is the human goal. Through his love for Krishna, King Parikshit attained liberation and entered divine existence."

Sadananda looked at me sadly. "Do you not understand? Are you still entangled in Shankaracharya's system, which you learned from Shri? Do you not see how terrible it must seem to a Bhakta that anyone can seek the love of God, as Shankaracharya has expounded it, as a means for attaining liberation? And then, if he has attained the knowledge, if he knows intuitively that he is one with the Brahman, he should let his love for God cool off and quiet down. Then he can take the picture of the personal God, which he no longer needs, and throw it in the river, as a final illusion. He himself is now the great Brahman."

"But in the story of Parikshit, it is said that he becomes the infinite Brahman. Is not becoming Brahman the highest goal?"

"No," said Sadananda shortly. "You know the verse from the last song in the *Bhagavad-gita*: '*brahmabhutah prasannatma*—he who has become one with the Brahman and has become one with his Atman, and no longer grieves, and no longer desires...' Well, continue reading it yourself."

I read: "...He attains the highest love, the highest Bhakti, for me."

"That means," explained my friend, "that he who has become one with the Brahman and has become one with the eternal spirit, and who no longer grieves and no longer desires, but who does not remain here, preferring in his great longing to serve and love ever more, to penetrate further—he attains the highest Bhakti for God. Krishna speaks thus. The final goal is not Mukti or liberation. The true Bhakta, like Parikshit, laughs at such an idea. Here in the *Bhagavata* it says, 'God bestows Mukti easily, but he seldom bestows Bhakti.' Spontaneous, unmotivated love of God, for love's own sake, is the highest human goal."

Sadananda came up to me and looked at me with flashing eyes. He seized me by the shoulders and shook me, reciting words from the Upanishads, so that they pierced me like lightning. "Arise! Awake, and do not cease until the goal is reached! Svasti!" Then he went away.

But still the crashing lightning of love penetrated my being, as if for a minute it tore away all earthly coverings from my innermost self.

CHAPTER XXII

THE STREAM OF DIVINE LOVE

Krishna, the first teacher of love—Brahma's song—Narada, the wanderer—Foundation of the world of Maya—The coming of Chaitanya

I sat in my shed at a table covered with papers. A mountain stream roared through the night. I thought of the stream of divine love, flowing inexhaustibly out of God's realm, flowing unnoticed by the great majority through our world of shadows.

Many Bhaktas say Krishna was the first guru to teach divine love. He performed the initiation for Brahma, who shaped the world according to God's plan. When Brahma awoke to new life after the long night of sleep called world dissolution—long before our world was created—he was surrounded by darkness. He did not know where he was. He did not know that he was in the calyx of a lotus flower whose stem grew out of the navel of Vishnu. The darkness stretched all around him. Troubled by this, Brahma arose and made his way upward in the calyx of the lotus. He wandered thus a thousand years, and yet reached no boundary. Still troubled, he turned back and wandered down towards the lotus stem for a thousand years; still he found no bottom.

Exhausted and discouraged, Brahma sat in the posture for meditation. When his heart had become perfectly quiet, he heard the sound of a flute, the tones of which awoke within him an overflowing love. It was the sound of Krishna's flute coming from his innermost kingdom. The tones were a mantra. Thus Brahma became initiated by God himself and came to be the first of all true Brahmans. From the mantra of divine love arose the four original

149

verses of the writing called *Bhagavata,* which later developed into 18,000 stanzas. As Brahma gazed into God's kingdom and longed for him, he remembered his identity and he felt capable of creating the universe. While he performed his difficult task, he sang a hymn with longing in his heart. Brahma sang of the divine world without fate, where no suffering lay at the bottom of every pleasure, where time is not painfully divided into past and present, where eternal presence prevails, and where everything is woven of love. Brahma sang of Krishna's kingdom:

> Every word is a song, every step a dance,
> and the flute, Krishna's beloved friend,
> resounds from his lips.
> Time, which flies so fast here,
> stands still there.
> Only a few of the wise who wander upon earth
> know of this land.

Brahma initiated his disciple and spiritual son Narada in divine love, and gave him the four original verses of the *Bhagavata.*

Shri and Sadananda had both told me about Narada, a great Bhakta who searches the world for souls who are ready to receive the strength for loving devotion to Krishna. Just as the sun shines on the righteous and unrighteous alike, the messengers of God wander about in their divine purity, and wherever they go they bring the radiance of God's kingdom. What does it matter to them whether the actions of a being are good or evil, according to the world's opinion, whether one is blessed or cursed? They see only the longing of the heart. What does it matter to them whether the ground they tread resembles a heaven or a hell? They enter prisons, madhouses, concentration camps. No murderer, no woman of the streets, no lunatic, no child in the mother's womb—none are excluded from the possibility of being welcomed into the circle of God's eternal companions.

In his wanderings, Narada once came to the dwelling of a hermit high up in the Himalayas, on the shore of a gushing river. There, near the source of the Ganges, sat the wise man Vyasa gazing depressedly into the whirling waters.

Vyasa greeted the messenger of God reverently.

"Why are you so sad?" asked Narada.

"There is something that I cannot understand," answered Vyasa in a troubled voice. "I have kept the law and practiced asceticism. I have mastered yoga better than all others. I have succeeded in collecting the books of the Vedas which were lost during the Great Flood. I have even finished the *Mahabharata* and the *Gita*. I have condensed the essence of Upanishadic wisdom in the Brahmasutras. I have meditated all of my life, and I have become one with the formless Brahman. And yet my soul is not at peace."

"In your beautiful works, you have spoken too much of the laws and logic of wisdom, and too little of God's love," Narada explained to him. "You must write yet another work that will bring divine love to humans."

Filled with compassion, Narada sang the mantra that Brahma had received from Krishna, and that he in turn had received from Brahma. Narada thus initiated Vyasa in divine love and gave him the four ancient verses of the *Bhagavata*.

Singing and playing his veena, Narada then went on his way. Vyasa sat on the shore of the young Ganges and meditated on the four verses. Now he saw Krishna in his innermost kingdom, and saw how the whole world of Maya has its foundation in Krishna. As Vyasa's heart gazed at Krishna, he burst into a song of praise, and rejoicing he began singing the stanzas of the work that speaks only of God, of Bhagavan, and which is therefore called *Bhagavata*. "The sweetest fruit on the tree of the Vedas, the nectar of immortality, a fruit without seed or skin"—thus the book is described.

Vyasa sang the numerous tales in the *Bhagavata* for his son, Shuka. The youth, who had lived in the kingdom of God since childhood, preserved the visions of Vyasa in his soul. Shuka in turn gave Parikshit love of God.

The initiation into divine love continued in an unbroken sequence through the centuries, from teachers to disciples and their disciples. Thus the revelation of God remained alive through the ages.

When Krishna descended to earth around the year 1500 A.D. as Krishna Chaitanya, he followed the venerable tradition by seeking a guru.

The guru immediately recognized the exalted being who had humbly approached him. Rejoicing, he initiated the avatar. Chaitanya departed reverently, and intoxicated with joy sang this stanza from the *Bhagavata* for three days: "Even I, even I shall stride through the terrible ocean of the changeable world and reach the other shore."

Chaitanya initiated his disciples into an entirely new stream of living words and divine love. And the stream of divine love flowed through India like the waters of life, hidden and yet not hidden, up to our own era. The hermit Gaura Kishora, a naked ascetic dressed only in a loin cloth, hardly able to read or write, gave the initiation to Bhakti-Siddhanta Sarasvati. He initiated a European disciple, whom he called Sadananda.

As I sat in the Indian prison camp, surrounded by noise and discord, Sadananda came and gave a drop of divine love—to me.

CHAPTER XXIII

THE PIGSTY

*A dream in prison—Who was Odysseus?—Singing Sanskrit verses—
Tūmpelbaum, the unwelcome newcomer—Circe's pigsty—Tricking
Circe, the enchantress—Fire in camp—Tūmpelbaum's change*

(Ulysses at the home of Circe)

Then by Athena the goddess,
the daughter of Zeus the Almighty,
taller and stronger to view he was made,
while down from his head fell
clustering thickly the locks of his hair,
as the flower hyacinth.

Odyssey, VI, 229–31

Thus when Athena had spoken,
her wand she extended and touched him;
all of the fair smooth flesh
on the limbs of his body she withered,
shrivelled the yellow hair from his head,
and the whole of his person,
every limb, with the skin
of a man right aged she covered.

Odyssey, XIII, 427–30

Spake, and her golden wand she extended,
and lo, as it touched him,

153

firstly a fair fresh mantle around him was cast,
and a doublet covered his breast,
and renewed was his body in stature and manhood;
dark once more was the tint of his skin,
and in face he was fuller;
blue-black bristled the beard
once more on his chin as aforetime.

Odyssey, XVI, 172–6

Even before the removal of our camp, I had a dream that set me thinking. I lay in darkness, as many times before, in the row of sleepers in the prison barrack. Those lying next to me were groaning in their sleep. I tried to remember the words of comfort in a Sanskrit hymn that my friend had written down for me. The words came back to me:

The knot of the heart shall be cut apart,
all doubt shall be torn away
and even his Karma,
his deeds and the inevitable consequences of his deeds,
shall disappear,
when he has beheld his Atman and God.

"What is the Atman?" I reflected. "As a man throweth away old garments and putteth on new, even so the soul in the body, having quit its old mortal frame, entereth into others which are new...." Thus it was written in the *Bhagavad-gita*. "This soul cannot be divided by weapons, the fire burneth it not, the water corrupteth it not, the wind drieth it not away, for it is all-pervading, inconceivable, eternal."

Moaning, my comrades turned again and again in their sleep, and the lousy wooden cots creaked. Often the room in the dark barrack was filled with a noise that made one think that a nightmare had seized the sleepers.

After a while I must have fallen asleep. In my dream I wandered through many lands, peeping curiously into all the holes of the earth, where wild animals attacked me. I ran through the night. The path became narrower and led steeply upward. I leaped through the air— below me were the clear, mighty waves of the sea. I fell and cried out.

From the depths of a great distance I heard the voice of my wife calling: "You are doing all that out of wantonness, *Odysseus!*"

I awoke at the sound of the word *Odysseus*. The rest of the night I lay thinking: Odysseus? I must find out more about Odysseus!

The next day I succeeded in finding a worn copy of a translation of Homer's *Odyssey*. Astonished, as if I were reading it for the first time, I read the familiar text that had been so dear to me in my boyhood, so dear that I had almost believed myself to have been present in the Greek camp at Troy and in Ulysses' tent and ship.

With a beating heart I read how Ulysses changed his form. His blond hair became dark like a hyacinth; his head was bald and later became covered with curly locks; he was old, became young, old again, and young again; his body grew in vigor, shriveled, became vigorous again; he was driven from shipwreck to shipwreck, even down into the region of the dead, and again up into the light. Ulysses, who constantly wore different clothes, those of a king, or those of a beggar, again those of a king, who was wrapped in a different body as the goddess waved her magic wand. The many tissues of lies, the many earthly careers that Ulysses tirelessly related—were they perhaps true? Was he born not only in Ithaca? Was he born in Crete and other places as well? As the *Bhagavad-gita* expresses it: "As a man throweth away old garments and putteth on new, even so the soul quitteth its worn body and enters another which is new."

Was I—was every soul on earth, like Ulysses—a wanderer from life to life?

I read on to the end, but the last page of the book did not end the wanderings of Ulysses. He was destined to wander farther, to a far-away mythical land where the stormy might of the wild sea—

his own mind's storm—would no longer reach him. But whether he succeeded in entering the kingdom of endless divine peace, which the Hindus call *shanti*, is not related in Homer's *Odyssey*.

The words of the last chapter of the book faded before my eyes. I had been reading outside in a corner of the sports field, and I had put on dark sunglasses to read in the blinding Indian daylight. Now the smoked glasses had become misty on the inside.

I took them off. Before me rose a wall of twisted wire, and beyond that a second one just like it. No, Odysseus was certainly not in the land of *shanti*, the kingdom of divine peace.

Guards strode backward and forward, bayonets raised, between the walls of iron thorns. Behind me there was noise and shouting. A football match was in progress. Somebody hit me between the shoulders with his fist. "Man, how can you sit there so unconcernedly!" My comrades cried indignantly, "How can anyone turn his back on a game like this! Think of it! The east barracks against the west barracks—the cup final!" He shook his head, as if doubting my sanity, and turned away.

Sadananda came joyfully to the corner of the field. The monk's gown, which he had dyed himself, gleamed brightly in the sun, as did his narrow ivory face and his clean-shaven head. "Come along, Vamandas," he smiled, calling me by my Indian name. "This game will soon be over. We can take a stroll."

The two of us strode slowly along the barbed-wire fence. Sadananda took me by the hand for a minute. "I see that your soul is deeply stirred. Have you noted the verse from the *Bhagavat-Purana* that I once recited for you?" I repeated in Sanskrit:

> The knot of the heart shall be cut apart
> when he has beheld his Atman and God.

My companion nodded assent and gave me a glance of approval. "You will master it. It is only the rhythm that must be improved. And it is not enough only to dream of the Atman; one must live in it, quite wide-awake."

As he moved, dancing rather than walking, Sadananda sang the Sanskrit verse once more.

Shrill whistles called us to the evening meal. We joined our comrades, who were hurriedly making their way toward the kitchen, tin plates in their hands.

Sadananda and I once celebrated a festival day in the toolshed. We sat beside each other on the newly scrubbed floor and sang Sanskrit verses, nearly a thousand years old, that praised Krishna, the hidden God.

But the last verse we sang was written by the Avatar of our own Dark Age, Krishna Chaitanya himself. My friend, who was usually so careful about demonstrating his feelings, now sang loudly and joyfully:

Not riches, not noble birth,
not beautiful women, nor the art of poetry,
do I desire, O Lord of the world.
But grant me birth after birth
unmotivated heartfelt love
O my God, unto thee!

A coarse voice, full of conceit and self-satisfaction, approached us angrily. A heavy body bumped up against the door of our shed, and somebody shouted, "Those confounded niggers and their swinish religion! They should be flogged to death!" Swearing and hurling insults, the man went on his way, filling the camp with his shouts.

The next day, this man, who was on good terms with one of the non-commissioned officers, obtained an order to move into the tool-shed as my roommate. He arrived panting, his boxes and bundles with him. His old trousers now decked my walls. His bed, with his dusty boots beneath it, now occupied the corner where Sadananda had sat singing God's name. The work table, which had been so difficult to put together, was now chiefly Tūmpelbaum's. It was no longer Sadananda who sat opposite me at this table, but Tūmpelbaum. When I looked up from my work, I looked into his spying, distended eyes. "Lock up all your things," Sadananda warned me. "When your are out, Tūmpelbaum will probably search your trunks."

The first time I opposed my new roommate, he came up to me, straddling, and standing so close that I could see every detail in his fat red face—the swollen mouth, the hanging underlip drawn into a crooked sneer, and his warm breath smelling of alcohol. He and I were at odds because he wanted to forbid Sadananda entrance to our shed. "Listen now," he shrieked. "Listen now, once and for all: That nigger is never to enter my door. You will soon see who is master in this room. Do you know what you are, you, you—you are a heathen! But I—I am a Christian!"

"You don't even know what religion, what Christianity, is," I said.

"I don't know what religion, what Christianity is?" Tūmpelbaum gasped for breath. Frothing with anger, he sat down.

"You must not let him get the upper hand!" Sadananda encouraged me. "You must master the situation. It must be possible for you to work in peace, even in the presence of this person."

"He is no human being," I burst out in my distress. "He is a dog that pokes his nose into everything. You have never spent a night by his side. The whole room is filled not only with the exhalations from his body, but even with the unclean sexual images that are always around him."

"Tūmpelbaum is not a dog—he is a pig," remarked Sadananda drily. "But you must not lose control of the matter. Hang up a blanket between your beds, so that his exhalations cannot reach you."

It was dark in the toolshed. Tūmpelbaum lay on his back, sleeping with his mouth open, snoring heavily. He must have adenoids in his fleshy nose, I thought. He should go to the hospital and let them cut the adenoids out of his snout! His breathing came in heavy gusts, like a storm at sea. I lay halfway between dreaming and waking. It was not in India now. Around me was the wind-swept sea described in the *Odyssey*.

While Tūmpelbaum snored like a pig, I walked in my dreams through the rotting forests of Homer's enchanted island Aiaie. About me the forest alternated between withered and green. The ground was hidden by mounds of mouldering leaves. I know that it was the forest that the Indians call Samsara, or the world of change. Enchanted animals looked at me with sorrowful eyes as I sought my companions, who had been turned into swine by the enchantress Circe.

Hermes, the Greek messenger of the gods, came toward me. Tall and slender, he moved swiftly with almost dancing steps. He took me by the hand kindly, and said:

> Whither, unfortunate, does thou wander
> alone in the highlands, strange to the place?
> It is surely thy comrades that yonder at Circe's
> closely imprisoned as pigs lie wallowing deeply in litter.
> Comest thou hither perchance to release them?

> Hermes pointed to the mounds
> of mouldering leaves lying on the ground:

> See here!
> Bearing this powerful charm,
> in the palace of Circe;
> enter—and thus from thy head
> shall be wended the day of destruction.
> Black at the root; but the flower
> was even as mild in its whiteness.
> Moly 'tis called by the gods,
> and to dig it is difficult labor,
> labor for mortals, I mean—
> but to gods are possible all things.

Not until now did I recognize the messenger of the gods who spoke to me. He wore an orange-colored Indian monk's gown. It was Sadananda. "Vamandas," he said, "Do you know what the word *moly* is in Sanskrit?"

"*Moly*—that is probably the word *mula:* root, source, ground."

"That is right," nodded Sadananda. "And who is the root of all things, their source, their ground?"

"Krishna," I answered without hesitating.

"And the shining flower?"

"That is of course the flower of the world, which grows up out of the hidden ground."

"Never forget for a minute that Krishna is the root of everything that exists," warned my friend. "Then the enchantress Maya cannot harm you."

He vanished on his light feet, and I wandered on toward the house that lay deep in the forest. A sweet song could be heard within, and the house shook as the enchantress worked her loom, weaving the web of the world.

How I laughed to myself as Circe opened the shining door with a welcoming smile, and invited me to come in and dine, slyly mixing the poison in my wine. I thought of the source of the world, the divine root, and drank fearlessly.

Laughing, the beautiful betrayer hit me with her staff, and commanded scornfully: "Off to the sty! Go crouch thee along with the rest of thy fellows!"

But he who possessed the root Moly could not be harmed by the poison of the sensual world. Circe shouted in amazement:

Surely I marvel that drinking the potion
thou feels not enchantment.
Never before hath a mortal resisted the potion
when once by the door of his teeth it had entered.
Surely within thy breast is a soul
too strong for bewitchment.

I rejoiced. "Happily, my heart is indestructible.
My inner heart is indeed an eternal soul."

I looked deep into the eyes of the enchantress Maya, and she revealed herself as she was. I recognized her, and she recognized the

Atman within me. I lay in her delightful bed, but she was powerless to do me any harm. Thus the night passed. The verses of the Odyssey streamed about me:

> While that the nymph threw round her
> a garment of glistening whiteness, delicate, lovely,
> and over her waist then fastened a girdle,
> beautiful, fashioned of gold,
> and her head in a hood she enclosed.

The colors of the earth were reappearing. Tūmpelbaum lay snoring in the morning light, his face swollen, his mouth drawn crookedly to one side. Had it been only a dream? Were we still in the pigsty? Must Tūmpelbaum and I, and all our comrades, be changed into real human beings? Through the open window I heard the whistling of the sleepy soldiers who paced between the two barbed-wire fences of the camp and signaled to one another. They were also enchanted, and were to carefully keep their enchanted comrades in their respective sties.

A fire broke out that day in one of the neighboring sections of the camp, that of the Italian fascists. The thatch roof of a large barrack was in flames. Fascinated by the sight, Tūmpelbaum stood close to the fence watching the fire and the crowd of prisoners who tried to save their few belongings. "All we need is a strong east wind," he shouted happily, "so that the whole camp can burn down, all of it." He stretched out his arms as if he would gladly welcome a fire that would destroy the whole world.

The fire seemed to strengthen Tūmpelbaum's self-assurance. As we sat in the shed, he excitedly announced how he would like to make a clean sweep of everything in the world. Corruption existed everywhere, he said, among the Allies as well as among the Axis powers. He raged against the Nazis and the Fascists; he raged against his own comrades, the anti-Nazis, with whom he shared the same barbed-wire cage, and who, in his opinion, were not true anti-Nazis. He showered his contempt on the Christian priests, the interned missionaries, the Jews and the few German and Italian Buddhists in the camp. Only he himself remained finally in solitary greatness. Licking his thick lips, he delightfully described how he would like to punish his opponents after the victorious conclusion of the war. "Pour melted lead into their mouths, skin them alive, hang them! You, too, you wretch, will be hanged," he prophesied with satisfaction.

"You, too, poor fellow, are a bewitched Atman," I thought. "But I must not forget that. I must always see the Atman in you."

Enraged at my silence, Tūmpelbaum began searching noisily for some tool in one of his trunks. He happened to pick up a framed photograph, the portrait of a little boy. He looked at the picture a long while, and then carefully nailed it up on the wall beside his bed. "My child, my little son who died when he was only three years old," he said, as he noticed the look of sympathy on my face. Then, quite unexpectedly, he began telling me about his youth in northern Germany, his disappointments and about the many trades he had tried in Siam, China, and other countries in the East. He had been a technician, a policeman, a teacher. He spoke of the mother of his dead son, an American nurse in the Philippines who had been taken prisoner by the Japanese. He knew nothing of her fate.

From that day my roommate's behavior toward me changed. "Good morning," he greeted me heartily and a bit rowdily every morning when he woke. He surprised me one day by laying some razor blades—a luxury in the camp—on the table, and asking me to accept them as a gift.

Tūmpelbaum even managed to behave politely towards Sadananda when the latter began coming again, quietly instructing me. But Tūmpelbaum was embarrassed in Sadananda's presence, and he usually vanished quickly from the shed, leaving us alone. This exaggerated courtesy, however, was not quite sincere.

"You had a visitor here while you were out. The doctor was here," he informed me once. Sadananda had come during my absence to fetch a Sanskrit book he had lent me. Tūmpelbaum followed my movements triumphantly as I searched among the books and manuscripts on my side of the table. "Aha! Is something missing?" he grinned. "The doctor carried something away with him. You must keep better watch over your friend!"

CHAPTER XXIV

THE MILK-WHITE GODDESS

On parole—Singing the Name of God in the woods—Following crowds of children—The temple of the Devi—Durga the jaileress

During the later years of our imprisonment, we were allowed to leave on certain days. For these "excursions on our honor," we were required to sign written agreements to return to the camp at a given time, and not to seek contact with any Indians. Violation of this agreement was punishable by a long jail term.

"Go out into the woods and sing the name of God," said Sadananda. "Even if you have not yet received initiation in God's name, you can sing it. You know so many of the names of God from the *Bhagavata* and other writings. Sing the names and put into the song all your longing to be able one day really to serve God in his own kingdom, in confident, loving devotion. Sing 'Krishna! Krishna! Krishna!' The vibrations of your song will move the sleeping Atman in stones, flowers, birds, and animals on your way, and their souls will awaken for a moment and remember their true nature: to love and serve God for all eternity. This is the redemption of the earth."

How wonderful it was to take these excursions with Sadananda! They were too few, however, for even then he was not well. After roll call on the sports field and at the exit, we went out through the two barbed-wire gates to the open road. We moved in single file along the narrow path between wet, flowering bushes that brushed up against our legs. We crossed the tall grass of the meadows fresh with morning dew and followed the river, whose waters flowed freely over the gravel during the rainy season. We waded bare-foot in the cold, crystal-clear water of the streams. It was easy to shake off and put on again the Indian sandals fastened with only a strap over the big toe. We walked through ripening wheat fields in which the stalks made one think of soldiers holding lances, as they beat against each other above our heads. To the north we glimpsed a mountain ridge now and then, behind the ears of grain or the leafy treetops.

I learned to see the world as my friend saw it. He taught me to love the Indian earth and the Indian rivers even more than I had done before. This land is sacred because divine saviors have traversed it since time immemorial; the rivers are sacred because their feet have waded through the waters.

"The true greatness of India lies neither in her natural wealth nor her great population, neither her art nor her history," explained Sadananda. "India's greatness lies in the fact that time after time, divine saviors, emanating from and returning to God, have chosen this land as a dwelling place. Only once has such a savior come to the West, overflowing with the power of God. Do you know who I mean?"

I nodded.

I thought of the holy bare feet that had walked through the waters of the Jordan River to the christening. I thought of how Christ's feet had wandered over the mountains of Galilee, over the temple courtyard of the great scholars, and over the hard cobble-stones in the narrow alleys of Jerusalem toward Golgotha.

From the nearby village a swarm of ragged children came run-ning toward us; they barred the road, begging, "Sahib, cigarettes! Sahib, cigarettes!" They knew that we had no cash. Sadananda laughed and gave them sweets instead of cigarettes. Before leaving for our excursions, he usually brought sweets for the children with the special paper money of the camp. And now he began to clap his hands and sing:

Raghupati Raghava Raja Ram
Patita Pavana Sita Ram

The whole troop of children marched along with us, singing and clapping. Years later, when Sadananda lay ill in the camp's hospital and I made these excursions alone, the children would come running toward me, asking, "Where is the Swami? Where is the Swami?" Then they would sing the song.

The singing of the children could be heard in the distance. Sadananda and I were resting near a spring. A Brahman came riding down a mountain slope on his donkey. When he reached the spring he dismounted, washed himself from top to toe, rinsed his mouth and drank, mumbling mantras the whole time. We knew he was singing the ancient formula to change the spring water into the same water as that which flowed in India's seven holy rivers:

> O Ganga! O thou Yamuna!
> Godavari! Sarasvati!
> Narbada! Sindhu! Kaveri!
> Make your dwelling in this water!

Sadananda also mumbled this invocation to the seven holy rivers before drinking. Without letting his hands touch the water, he took the running water into his mouth. He bathed in a crevice below a little fall. Diving and rising, spurting and spouting, he sang gaily while he bathed, " 'Shivo'ham, shivo'ham'—I am Shiva, I am Shiva! I, like Shiva, am Krishna's servant." Many Bhaktas in India worship Shiva not as the Lord of the world, the Lord of the yogis, or as the Destroyer, but rather as the ideal Bhakta. In his innermost self, Shiva is a Bhakta of God who meditates on Krishna with the deepest longing. Old legends tell that the walls in the house of Shiva, Kailas, are bright with frescoes that depict scenes from the life of Krishna.

Near a group of aging lingam stones, raised in honor of Shiva, stood a ramshackle resting place for pilgrims and a temple dedicated to Maya, who is often called simply Devi, the goddess. The sanctuaries of Shiva and Maya usually stand near one another. The temple, surrounded by mighty mango trees, lies on the old pilgrim road leading from the city of Hardvar to the source of the Yamuna River high up in the regions of eternal snow. There the great mistress of the universe bears a name that I had heard nowhere else in India: Dudhya Devi, the Milk-White Goddess. This brought to mind my dream of Odysseus, and the strange words Homer makes the messenger of God say to the wandering Odysseus: "Milk-white is the flower…" Here Maya is worshiped as the milk-white mistress of the life of all the worlds.

I thought of her as the goddess Arbuda with the black countenance, before which I had stood with Shri in the cave inside Mt. Abu. And I thought of her as the giant, blood-red Kali in the gloomy mountain cave. Now I stood before her once again, where she had entered into daylight. She was enveloped in only a thin veil, and this time her color was milk-white. But everywhere she was the same mysterious Maya.

According to the Indian custom, Sadananda walked three times, following the course of the sun, around the stone wall of Devi's temple, and I followed. She is worshiped under many names by those who pray for earthly gifts—sons, riches, liberation from sickness.

Sadananda sat with his legs crossed a long while in the cool temple, around which Himalaya stretched in all its loveliness, with its steep, forest-clad slopes, its torrents and ravines. He sang to the great Maya. It seemed as if he conversed with her.

"What did you sing to Maya?" I asked on our way home, as we walked through the forest, over meadows and grassy slopes, down the steep hills to the barbed-wire camp. "One of her many names is Durga, which means prison. I have told Durga, the jaileress, who serves Krishna in exile, about Krishna's hidden kingdom, which she herself does not dare to approach."

I stopped short in my amazement. The stones under my feet crumbled into gravel.

Sadananda continued: "I told Durga about Radha, who is the personification of God's power of rejoicing, and who serves Krishna with inexpressible love in his inner kingdom. Thus can a Bhakta of

Krishna honor the great Maya, and bring her joy. For she is a devoted servant, a shadow of Radha."

At the camp, dusty crowds of homecomers gathered before the sentry box at the entrance; our names were called and noted. A guard unlocked the double-barred gate for us, and once more we were confined within the walls of barbed wire.

CHAPTER XXV

THE HOLY NIGHT

Winter in the Himalaya region—Christmas celebrations—The poetry of Novalis—Meditations on the Nativity—Parallel of the Indian legend—Jesus and Krishna—The wanderings of Chaitanya—The avatar of the future

Winter nights at the foot of Himalaya are cold and stormy. Tümpelbaum and I often froze miserably in our draughty shed. The three oblong windows still had no glass. On Christmas Eve, Tümpelbaum left early to celebrate in more pleasant surroundings at a drinking bout with fellows of his own kind. The way was clear for Sadananda to visit me.

My little retreat was decidedly colder than Sadananda's barrack, where a fire burned gaily in an open fireplace. Yet he preferred to come to my cold room so that I did not spend the holy night in loneliness.

When my friend arrived, he was shivering with cold, for he did not own an overcoat. Even in winter he went about clothed only in his thin, orange-colored cotton gown. I wrapped him in blankets, and, as so often before, we sat opposite each other at the rickety table. We spoke of the savior whose blessed birth was being celebrated this cold night all over the world. Sadananda loved Christ and I loved Christ, but Sadananda knew him better, for he knew the ever-living Christ.

"Vamandas, take a notebook and a pencil and write," he said to me. And then I received a favor I had once asked of him. He compared the worship of God by both Christians and Indian

Bhaktas. First he spoke of the courage of faith (*Wagnis des Glaubens*), in the West as well as in India. He spoke of the simplicity of child-like devotion in Bhakti and in Christianity, and of the sacrifice of worldly esteem (*Einsatz der Achtung der Welt*), the complete change of personality in human beings (*Verwandlung des ganzen Menschen*), the meaning of brotherhood (*Bedeutung der Gemeinschaft*) and the sanctity of life....It was the essence of a whole scientific book, perhaps even a whole life's work, that he dictated to me that night in short, forcible sentences.

From one of the barracks came the sound of a little bell. It was the Protestant Christmas service. A few hours later the ringing of a bell was heard in another barrack; it was the Catholic midnight mass. But the bells and the stillness of the night were repeatedly interrupted by disturbances. Most of the guards from England and its dominions were drunk, and so were most of the prisoners. The wild clamor of drunken persons penetrated our wall from the barracks and the canteens in the various barbed-wire enclosures and from the dark landscape outside the barbed wire.

"The poor fellows cannot solve their many problems and troubles, and therefore they get drunk," said my friend sympathetically.

The door was wrenched open and a strong gust of wind rushed in. My corpulent roommate staggered into the room. Without seeming to notice our presence, Tūmpelbaum vomited several times, and then threw himself on his bed with all his clothes on, not even bothering to remove his boots, and began to snore.

Sadananda calmly continued as before, sitting at the table. Neither the noise outside, nor the sounds emitted by the sleeping drunkard affected us. We enjoyed a happy, festive silence for a while. "What are you thinking about, Vamandas?" my friend asked earnestly a little later.

I recited slowly some lines by Novalis, which I had loved since boyhood:

> *Ein Gott für uns, ein Kind für sich,*
> *liebt er uns all herzinniglich.*

170

Aus Kraut und Stein, aus Meer und Licht
schimmert sein kindlich Angesicht.

A smile lit Sadananda's face. "It is fine, Vamandas, that you have brought just those lines from Europe to India." He got up and looked at me with shining eyes. "But do you remember the prophetic verse that the seer Novalis placed before the lines you repeated just now?"

I continued gladly:

Geuss Vater ihn gewaltig aus.
Gib ihn aus deinem Arm heraus!

We remained silent. Then Sadananda placed of both his hands on my shoulders for a minute. "I must go now. Think of him who on a troubled night like this descended to the dark earth. A blessed Christmas to you, Vamandas!" With light footsteps he vanished into the blackness of the night.

While my comrade Tūmpelbaum slept off the effects of his drunkenness, hawking and gurgling beside me, I lay on my hard bed, completely happy. I thought of the child that nearly two thousand years ago had been born in a manger, because every house and every inn of the little town of Bethlehem was overflowing with boisterous guests. Joseph and Mary had bent over the newborn child, humbly and fearfully. The words spoken by the angel were imprinted in the heart of the divine Mother. The animals in the stable breathed quietly beside the humble cradle of the child. Hardly anybody suspected that the long-awaited son of God had at last arrived. Only a few poor shepherds, led by divine voices, came and worshiped the child. And three wise men from the East brought him gifts.

I pondered the particulars of the sacred story, which is known to all of us. But I thought, too, of another holy child who was born in India thousands of years earlier. That child, too, entered the world on a dark midnight, and the scene of his coming was even more lamentable than the stable in Bethlehem. The Krishna child

171

was born in a prison. His father and mother were chained to the prison wall with heavy iron links. Wicked King Kamsa, who resembled Herod, the dismal king of the Jews, had killed all of Krishna's brothers, for it had been prophesied that a son of these parents would one day dethrone and slay him.

The *Bhagavata* relates that Vasudeva, Krishna's father, received the divine child first in his spirit; he then communicated the divine being to the spirit of his young wife Devaki. While she bore the holy child, her radiance illuminated the whole house, and the demoniacal king was seized with terror. When the boy was born, the parents recognized his divine majesty, and they fell to their knees, singing hymns in his praise.

Although Devaki knew well that eternal, almighty God was embodied in her son, her heart was filled with fear. She anxiously pleaded with the newborn child, "Oh! Hide your divine majesty, so that the terrible king cannot see who You are." Krishna obeyed the anxious mother and assumed the form of a helpless human child.

The exhausted mother fell into a deep sleep, and the father took the child in his arms. At Krishna's command, his chains fell away, the prison gates opened, and Vasudeva walked past the sleeping guards out into the dark night. His heart knew which way he should go. The swollen Yamuna River parted for him so that he could walk with dry feet between the roaring walls of water. He reached the opposite shore unharmed and continued towards the pastoral village Vraja, still carrying the child. Here, too, all were asleep, including the cowherd king Nanda. Queen Yashoda, having just given birth to a daughter, was sleeping deeply, and did not know whether she had given birth to a boy or a girl that night.

Vasudeva carefully laid Krishna on her breast and took the baby girl in his arms. He returned the same way that he had come, and laid the little girl in the arms of his sleeping wife. The gates of the prison were locked once more behind him. When the child began to cry, the stupefied guards awoke and rushed to the king with the news that he had fearfully expected.

Filled with grim determination, King Kamsa burst into the prison, seized the newborn child by the feet, and threw it against the stone wall. But the child vanished in smoke. From every direction, through the enchanted night, a laugh reached the ears of King Kamsa. And in the laugh he discerned a voice: "You wretch! You thought you could kill *me*! I am Maya. All this has happened by the will of God. Krishna is in safe hands. Woe to you, King Kamsa. You shall not escape destruction."

The two stories now became interwoven. Trembling before the wrathful King Herod, who commanded that all the newborn children in Bethlehem should be killed, Mary and Joseph fled with their child to Egypt. Jesus was safe. The child was taken to the temple of God, and old Simeon recognized the promised Messiah. He took him in his arms and cried out joyfully: "Lord, allow Thy servant to go forth in peace, for my eyes have beheld Thy splendor."

Krishna grew up safely in the land of the cowherds, although Kamsa sent his mighty demons across the river to destroy him. As soon as Krishna touched them, their terrible bodies fell dead. At the same time, these horrible creatures were saved by the touch of Krishna's hand, or his little feet or his childish mouth. Before the eyes of all, they entered into his divine light.

Many other tales told in the *Bhagavata* about Krishna's childhood awoke in my memory. The little boy once sat on Yashoda's lap, and as always, she was filled with love as she looked at Krishna. Satisfied with his meal of mother's milk, the child yawned sleepily. When the mother looked into the child's open mouth, she beheld to her surprise the whole earth, the sun, the moon, and the starry skies. "Who are you, Krishna?" she asked wonderingly. The child closed his mouth again and smiled up at her. And overwhelmed with maternal love, Yashoda immediately forgot what she had seen and fondled and kissed little Krishna.

Another time, Yashoda was going to punish Krishna by binding his waist; the little boy had crept up on a stool and broken a pot of butter. After eating his fill, he had also shared it with the cat and the monkeys. But Yashoda's rope to was too short, and her clothes line did not suffice, either. She tied an extra bit to it, but the cord was not long enough. Soon, all the neighboring women stood around her laughing at her efforts to bind Krishna's little waist. Then the boy, who stood in a corner crying, saw that his mother was sweating and trembling from her efforts. He, the Eternal One, whose infinity the greatest yogis and wise men have been unable to fathom, felt sorry for his mother. Krishna then became an obedient child and allowed himself to have his waist bound by one who loved him so much.

The door of the toolshed was jerked open. Three drunken men stuck their heads through the opening. "Tūmpelbaum! Tūmpelbaum! Tūmpelbaum! Come and have another drink!" they shouted. Tūmpelbaum only grunted in his sleep and rolled onto his other side. The men began hoarsely singing a vulgar street song; then they slammed the door and tottered on, supporting one another, intending to repeat their performance at the next barrack.

The stories of how God descended to earth are entwined: The hidden savior about whom the West knows nothing was also born at midnight. A full moon illumined the earth, but a lunar eclipse was approaching. The bright disc of the night sky darkened as people began to sing. Many reverently entered the Ganges to bathe, and, according to ancient tradition, to invoke God during the eclipse. Just then Krishna Chaitanya was born. Wrapped in the name of God, the sound of which caused the firmament to tremble, Krishna Chaitanya came to the world.

Like the birth of Christ, his appearance had been predicted many centuries before, by holy men and prophets.

An old man had prayed for many years that the golden avatar might descend. When the child was born, crowds of strangers are said to have streamed joyfully to the house of the amazed father, falling on their knees before the child and bringing him rich presents. According to legends, these strangers were Brahma, Shiva, and other exalted heavenly beings in disguise. Neighbors and friends of the mother came to her with gifts. In order to test the character of the newborn child, they placed before him jewels, coins, silks, a clod of earth, and lastly a book, the *Bhagavata*. Without hesitating, the boy grasped at the book in which God's deeds of love are praised, put his arms about it and clasped it to his breast.

Dancing and singing, Chaitanya made his way through India, from the Ganges to Cape Comorin in the south. Faded trees became green again as he passed. The animals of the forest recognized him and followed him. And everyone who met or saw him was overwhelmed with the love of God—simple men, learned philosophers of the school of Shankaracharya, Buddhist and Mohammedan beggars, the casteless, Brahmans, ministers, princes, and the ruler of a mighty kingdom. When two notorious robbers tried to murder him, infuriated when he and a whole city sang the name of God, they too became filled with overwhelming love and began singing the divine name.

Krishna Chaitanya did not perform miracles. He slew no demons, and seldom do we hear of his having healed the sick or raised the dead. But he cured thousands of people of the most terrible suffering—the illness of not knowing love. I repeated softly to myself the mantra that Sadananda had taught me:

> Praise to the most generous one,
> to thee who bestowest love for Krishna,
> to thee Krishna called Krishna Chaitanya,
> who shines like molten gold.

For forty-eight years Chaitanya wandered upon earth, as Bhaktas say, "Wrapped in Radha's bright beauty and her love of God." He longed inexpressibly for Krishna. Then one day he vanished; apparently, he re-entered Krishna.

Many villages in Bengal still sing his songs and some await his return, which he promised. For four hundred years they have been waiting for him, and in the evenings they sing and watch for him.

Others also await the savior, the promised avatar of the future. The whole world is secretly waiting for him to descend from heaven.

175

Toward dawn, the disturbance outside quieted down. Was it singing that I heard, the singing of Christmas songs? "Silent night, holy night…"

The tales of saviors from the East and the West stretched their branches above me like blooming rose bushes from the same root:

> Ein Gott für uns, ein Kind für sich,
> liebt er uns all herzinniglich.
>
> Aus Kraut und Stein, aus Meer und Licht
> schimmert sein kindlich Angesicht.
>
> Geuss Vater ihn gewaltig aus.
> Gib ihn aus deinem Arm heraus!

That night it seemed as if I had lived all my life at the bottom of a deep well, longingly looking up at the little bit of sky visible through the hole at the top. I saw a beloved star there. It was called Christ. But now I began to climb up the sides of the well. The star was shining nearer and brighter, with more and more love, and now it was no longer alone. Other saviors were shining all around it, a whole starry heaven of God's fathomless love. Their light streamed down toward me. The saviors who descended to earth, one after another, seemed to be different. They were shining with varying radiance and strength. Some were heavily veiled, others less so. And yet they were not really different. All were revelations of the Only One. They all originated from the same ancient light, the same original divine being.

I do not know if I gradually fell asleep or if I was still awake. It seemed to me, however, that I stood before the promised avatar of the future, who was pure light and love. "What is your name?" I asked. "My name is, 'I am coming,'" he answered.

CHAPTER XXVI

THE GATE OPENS

Sadananda falls ill—Engineering a visit to hospital—Lines from the Padma-Purana explained—Why I had come to India—The hidden purpose of the prison camp—Sadananda hovers between life and death—Translating the Bhagavata—He comforts the hospital menials—He fasts, then decides to live—World history in the making—The escapists—News from my wife—I dream of release—Sadananda set free—A letter from Shri

When Sadananda handed me a bundle of loose sheets from the *Padma Purana* wrapped in a silk cloth, he was already very ill in the camp hospital. This was after the first abdominal operation, when the doctors were convinced that he was going to die. I had managed to get a look at him now and then through the window. He lay there emotionless and pale like a corpse in a room known among the patients as the "death room." But one day, to my surprise and delight, I received a note written by Sadananda himself. "*My dear Vamandasji, do not remain in God's antechamber, in the infinite light of the formless Godhead. For the true Krishna never enters that place...*" It was signed, "Always in the one service: Sada."

A postscript was added: *Vamandasji, can't you visit me sometimes here in the hospital?*

It was strictly forbidden for we who were interned to visit anyone in the hospital, but with a little ingenuity I managed this the following day. I complained of serious eye trouble and was sent to the hospital under escort for treatment.

The old eye doctor was one of our comrades, a prisoner like ourselves. He had been the favorite pupil of a world-famous professor at a German eye clinic, and had been sent to the Dutch Indies for scientific study. The First World War had prevented his returning home, and he had remained on the wealthy island of Java even after the war was over. As superintendent of a sanatorium, he had gradually managed to forget the ambitious dreams of his youth, and he had sunk into the pleasant life of the tropics. The white-haired old man wrote according to form in his card system, noting down the details in regard to my person. Then with skillful fingers he lifted my eyelids, smeared them with a silver preparation and other drugs, and at my own suggestion decided that I should return the next day for further treatment.

"Why, Vamandas! What a sorry sight you are!" exclaimed Sadananda with a laugh that turned into a grimace of pain. He stretched out his thin hand to me warmly. "What is the matter with your eyes? Tears are running down and leaving black streaks on your face!"

"My eyes have been treated with *lapis infernalis*."

"Is there something wrong with them?"

"Nothing at all."

"I see, you have done this in order to enter the hospital and visit me. That is very kind of you."

During the short half-hour that I sat beside Sadananda's bed, he told me many hidden truths. Finally he gave me the lines about Krishna's inner kingdom from the *Padma-Purana* to translate. They were the same lines that he had sung some months previously for the milk-white goddess during one of our long walks in the forest.

The *Padma-Purana* originates from the ninth century, but it is based partly on an oral tradition that is much older, passed on for innumerable generations, from guru to disciple. The translation was very difficult. The text was printed in a very old-fashioned way; the words were not separated from one another, but each line of verse was forged into one block of words. And where the various words melted into one another, the sounds were changed and had been assimilated. It often required long, patient listening to the rhythm of the lines and their inner significance before their meaning became clear.

While I translated, my roommate sat at the far end of the room. Without saying a word, he had given up his share of the table, and had made himself a new one out of an old box. He now felt more at ease and could engross himself in his favorite occupation, solving mathematical problems and geometrical figures. It was very hot, surely more then 100 degrees in the shade, and the flies were pestering him. They were attracted to his perspiring, red face. Tūmpelbaum kept hitting at his tormentors with a fly-killer, which he thwacked many hundreds of times angrily, not far from my neck. This did not bother me, however. As carefully as I could, I wrote down the words of revelation that Krishna, the hidden God, had spoken as He smilingly addressed his devoted Bhakta, Shiva.

I felt as if I were wandering in an unknown land, on a path toward a distant mountain. At first, the mountain appeared like a solid, bright blue wall of clouds. Upon closer inspection, it developed into a landscape of hills and valleys, woods and lakes, and one met the beings who lived there. In the same way, the veiled kingdom of divine love reveals itself gradually to the devoted soul.

This is no dream; it is not poetry. It is pure reality. A gleam from the eternal realm of archetypes has always penetrated my life. Even as a boy, I often awoke frightened, as if I had been rescued after a long, endless wandering: I have forgotten something, I have forgotten something infinitely important!

I had to travel to India to regain what I, and all of us, have forgotten and lost; to the land where there is no guilt and no fate, where that which has been done will be undone. The ground there is not earthly soil. Time there is not earthly time—every moment is no longer divided into past and future. There, happiness is not always tinged by sorrow. There is no death. "Each word is a song, each step a dance...." But one cannot enter with selfish motives; only through

SADANANDA

unselfish devotion can one reach this land. One must travel mountains of night before the first morning ray of the veiled land.

When I first set out for this realm—open to all, yet thickly
veiled from our sight—and kept stumbling, my life was filled to the
brim with the utmost despair. Yet in a world of barracks—where
everything of spiritual value that I had once attained seemed lost,
where every path ended in a tangle of barbed wire, and where going
farther might mean death—I tried to make my way on the path to a
land without guilt or fate.

Sadananda helped me find the open gate to Vraja, where one
can proceed eternally without coming to an end. Now I know that it
was only to find him that I had undertaken the journey to India. I
would have gladly searched the world, but I had to find him in a
prison camp.

Sadananda was laid on the operating table five times during his
imprisonment. Each time he placed himself completely in the hands
of God. Once, before awakening from his unconscious state, he sang
"Krishna, Krishna, Krishna!" for an hour without stopping. The medical attendant, one of our comrades, asked him afterward why he had
called that name incessantly. Sadananda became embarrassed,
ashamed that he could not hide his heart better.

For about two years my friend lay in the camp hospital, with
only short intervals of respite. Several times he was placed in the
room for the dying. I often sat beside his bed in one of the wards. My
real instruction began at this time, when I had to fight for every
opportunity to see him.

Even in the hospital, Sadananda worked much of the time.
When I arrived, I usually found him sitting with his legs crossed on his
bed. His little metal trunk lay on his knees, serving as a table, and he
wrote eagerly. Often, however, I found him sleeping, his head under
the sheet, resting after a sleepless night of pain. All about him in the
hospital there was noise and disturbance. I waited calmly until he awoke.

When we were together, he looked over the translations I had
completed since our last meeting. He often criticized me, complain-

ing that I worked too fast and not precisely enough. "Nobody expects you to be a racer," he once said to me. "One can speed on tracks of dead gravel and ashes. But on the spiritual pastures of the *Bhagavata,* where God and his friends play their eternal games, one should tread with reverence." "You must bow down inwardly before every line of a verse, every word, as if they contained the final revelation. And then you must remain quiet, listening, until the original text itself takes the initiative within you and begins expressing itself."

He once warned me, "A notebook containing translations of the *Bhagavata* should be a model of neatness and order. This order attracts Krishna's grace. Each pencil, each sheet of paper, can be a means of serving Krishna and bringing him joy. My guru insisted on such order, which colors all of one's life, and he was an example of what he preached. Like all Hindus, he ate with his fingers. But he touched his food only with the tips of his fingers. It was not like eating, when he partook of a meal, but rather like praying."

For a long time Sadananda observed a pledge of complete silence, writing his answers and remarks on bits of paper. In this way many of his utterances have been preserved, and I treasure them.

One day he asked me, "Why are you so upset, Vamandas? It troubles me."

Then I told him that a cat had been killed in the camp, just before we on the sick list had marched to the hospital. "A crowd surrounded the cat, which was not quite dead yet. It wanted to creep away and hide, as animals do when they know they are going to die; it tried to get up and escape to some dark corner, but it sank down whining again and again. Its back was broken. I did not know what to do. Should I have taken a stone and thrown it at the cat to end its misery? I did nothing. I just went away. What should I have done?"

Sadananda's eyes flashed. His whole being was afire. "You behaved quite wrongly, Vamandas. You should have knelt beside the dying animal, in spite of all the staring eyes about you, and sung Narasimha's mantra in the ear of the animal. You know that I have given you that mantra, the verse about Krishna's great avatar

Narasimha, who tears away the veil of Maya from the soul like a spiritual lion with diamond claws, and wakes it to life. If you had done this, the animal would have been reminded in the hour of its death that it is an Atman, belonging only to Krishna; and that its inner mission is to serve Krishna for all eternity."

Sadananda was loved by the Indian boys who performed the most menial work in the hospital, that of emptying night chambers, and the like, for the European prisoners. It made him very unhappy when one of the German internees once tried to incite the boys against him. But they took no notice of this. He, the European Mahatma, understood their language. He instructed them regularly as they sat about him, listening to him describe the descent of Krishna and the great avatars. The superintendent of the hospital forbade this instruction and demanded heavy fines from the poor boys, but they kept coming to him with their troubles. He paused whatever work he was doing, for their sake. He always had time for them. He even helped these boys, who were excluded from schools, in their patient efforts of learning to read and write. Every time I visited the hospital I saw one or two of these boys sitting in the narrow strip of shade outside the toilet houses, squatting on their heels, ready in case the gruff voice of any sick sahib called them. They held a pad of writing paper and a reader on their knees, and tried to copy the involved figures of Hindi script.

In the hospital, in the whole camp, and in the bazaars of the neighboring communities, the rumor began to spread that Swami Sadananda had begun fasting. He preferred to die rather than be forced to continue eating meat. After one of the operations, the German doctors tried to persuade him to drink *bouillon*. I had often witnessed the agony he experienced, when he was forced to choose between starvation and forbidden food. He had tired of this. Although still very weak after his severe surgery, he had begun to fast. The hospital attendants were instructed to serve his meals punctually and leave the food beside his bed until it was time for the next meal.

Not until the evening of the sixth day of his hunger strike did I succeed in entering the hospital as a patient. When I came into his room, he was so weak that he could only acknowledge my presence with his eyes. I was sure I was looking at my friend for the last time.

Suddenly, he began speaking in a clear, surprisingly forceful voice. He gave me a familiar command: "Vamandas, take a pencil and paper and write. I shall dictate to you a Sanskrit prayer from the *Padma-Purana*. It is directed to the divine pair, Radha-Krishna, the two who are one."

> That which is I, that which is mine,
> in this world, in a future life—
> May all this be borne today
> as a sacrifice before your feet.
> I am thine, Krishna! I am thine, Radha!
> With my body and all my deeds,
> with my spirit, and with every word
> my tongue speaks.

When Sadananda finished, I asked him, "Swamiji, don't you really wish to live a little longer?"

He smiled, and said humorously, "Yes, today when I saw you walk past my window, I decided to live a little longer, to continue the instruction I have begun giving you, before you are capable of making your way alone."

My friend broke his fast. We reached a new stage of companionship that evening.

While I received my instruction, almost unperceived by my comrades, world history was in the making. On four continents, the war fronts were pushed forward and withdrawn again. These changes cast heavy shadows over our camp, where everything continued seesawing up and down. Men who had previously been disregarded suddenly became influential personalities in the barracks;

those who had been highly respected and greeted with flattery sank among the masses, degenerated, and disappeared. One year followed another. We began to get gray and lose our teeth. I once happened to stand in the queue behind a man who had always been exceedingly particular about his appearance. Now I saw a bedbug walk calmly from the collar of his ragged khaki shirt, and down his back. As the years went by, he had converted everything he owned into drink, even his fine suits that were made by a well-known English tailor. The members of the camp celebrated every little victory with a drinking bout, and they drank again to drown their sorrow after a defeat.

A group of mountain climbers, taken unaware by the outbreak of war during an expedition in Himalayas, could no longer stand the confinement behind the barbed wire. They succeeded in carrying out a well-planned escape. Some of them got far away into Tibet, but some were captured; we saw them in the camp after they had served a term in the camp prison. Others, ill with fever, had dragged themselves through the mountain tracts and voluntarily given themselves up to the police. One of them who had held out the longest told me that toward the end he could not bear the loneliness of Tibet's windy desert plateau: the roaring of the storm, the rushing of the torrents in the mountain crevices, and above all the strange thoughts that stole over him at night. He told of the greed of the people there, their desire for silver coins. He spoke of a deserted village uninhabited by even a single living person, and of a village nearby, where he had been driven away by stoning as he approached it, tired and hungry. He showed me a deep scar on his forehead that he had received on this occasion. "Not until later did we find out that a few villages near Lake Manasarovar had been completely depopulated by the ravages of smallpox. The people in the village where we were stoned were beside themselves with fear that we were contaminated," he said.

I was horrified. I had come to India to cross Himalaya and reach Lake Manasarovar, and now I understood that even in these regions human beings hated one another, and suffered fear, greed, and sickness. Oh! It was just as Shri had said. The lake of the Holy Ghost is not to be found on earth; it lies in quite another world.

I was sitting beside the bed of my friend in the hospital when I received a card from my wife, sent from Sweden. I had known for a while that she and our child had found sanctuary in the eleventh hour in this hospitable country. My wife wrote: *We must thank God that your beloved mother is dead, that she need no longer suffer in the ghetto camp of Theresienstadt.*

I bowed my head. My mother had been a proud, fiery soul. There was no egoism in her. She had had only one last wish in life: to see her son once more. This great longing had kept her alive for years in an environment in which the majority succumbed. But the fulfillment of this one burning wish had been denied her.

I could not prevent the tears from streaming down my face. Some of the patients in the ward noticed this and stared curiously. Sadananda took my hand, "Vamandas, your mother is with Krishna, in Krishna's realm," he said comfortingly.

The next time I visited Sadananda he told me of a dream he had had: "I dreamed that I was released from the camp, but when I went out through the gate to travel to Brindaban, where a friend, a disciple of my guru, lives, I was stopped by the guard. He said to me, 'Yes, you may go. But you must take the little child with you.'" Sadananda smiled. "It was a bright, healthy youngster, but its eyes and ears were sealed with earth. Vamandas, do you know who that child was?"

Oh, I knew. It was myself. It was my spiritual eyes and ears that were sealed with earth. Whimsically, but at the same time with my heart quietly rejoicing, I answered with a mantra he had taught me:

> I bow with reverence to the guru who opened my eyes, as if with a little staff smeared with the salve of wisdom, and took away the darkness of my blindness.

We both laughed. "We have some way to go as yet, before getting that far," Sadananda remarked.

Shortly afterward, Sadananda was suddenly given his freedom. He traveled to Brindavan, the region which, according to the conviction of many Bhaktas, reflects the brightness of Krishna's inner kingdom. There, on the shores of the Yamuna River, Krishna had spent his happy youth among the cowherds.

Although every bed but his was occupied, the hospital ward seemed empty when Sadananda left. Kahosta, formerly a ladies' hairdresser from Vienna who had introduced permanent waving successfully among the young Chinese women of Haza, glanced disdainfully at his remaining comrades in the ward, and said, "It's awfully dull here now that the Hindu fellow has left us. All of us miss him."

But I was happy and full of confidence. I was sure that I would see my friend again. There was only one thing that troubled me, and that was the complete silence for so many years of my first guru, Shri. Was he silent because he felt that in many ways I had been unfaithful to him? He had wanted to lead me to the exalted goal of knowing the *truth*. But during my association with Sadananda I had learned that unless one's heart overflows with the love of God, the greatest wisdom is nothing but chaff, like empty husks which it is useless to try to thresh.

I wrote a letter to Shri, trying to describe in detail the inner evolution I had experienced. For several years he had observed a pledge of silence. He neither wrote nor spoke. He only meditated for the harassed world. But now he broke his pledge. I received a letter in his own handwriting. Shri wrote:

> My dear Vamandasji!
> You have spent your time in India well. I bless you.
> I bless you for what you have done. And I bless you
> for what you are going to do in the future.

A few days after receiving this missive, I was quite unexpectedly released from the prison camp. As I passed through the two iron-barred gates, the guard asked as usual, "To the hospital?" The English non-commissioned officer escorting me answered, "No, he is free." There were still several thousand men behind the barbed wire of the camp.

CHAPTER XXVII

A FAREWELL TO INDIA

Good-bye to prison—I visit Shri in Mahabaleshvar—Alone in Bombay—Gandhi is welcomed by vast crowds—His son sings—Sadananda's visit—I am initiated by Swami Bon—Embarkation for Europe—I fly from London to Sweden—Reunited with my family

When I left the camp, the first visit I made was to Shri. He had retired to the mountain regions of Mahabaleshvar, where I once had spent a summer with him. Just as before, I sat at the feet of the good old man. He kept the pledge of silence he had held for so many years. But every morning and evening, when I bowed deeply before him, he stroked my hair with his slim hand, by way of blessing, and looked down kindly at me with his child-like, innocent, happy smile. Rana was also there, and once again he and I wandered together in the woods, where wonderful orchids grew on the trees. Now and again we would be surprised by a glimpse of deep valleys and ravine in the open spaces between the foliage of the trees, and sometimes even a glimpse of the faraway sea.

From Mahabaleshvar I traveled to Bombay to obtain a boat reservation to Sweden. It had been more than eight years since I had seen my family, and my courageous wife had carried the burden of responsibility all this time. Now she had nearly reached the end of her strength. She had written: "Come and take care of our child."

I was quite alone in Bombay as I hastened from one government office to another, filling out long questionnaires to prove that my journey was necessary. Not only myself, but whole armies that had fought in Asia were waiting for a chance to get home. Sadananda and his friend, Swami Bon, had traveled to Assam, on the farther end of India near the Chinese border. I had written to him that I would like to meet him once more, but to what avail were letters or telegrams when the whole of India had been paralyzed for weeks by a general post and telegraph strike? Unforwarded letters and telegrams lay in heaps on the floors of empty post offices. There was a rumor of a railway strike as well. Bank clerks, who demanded a salary raise, were distributing flyers on the streets instead of sitting at their counters. Long columns of demonstrators sometimes marched through town with bright red banners that bore the hammer and sickle. Bombay had changed decidedly since I landed there. Only the shrill chorus of voices from the gold exchange remained the same.

One day I read in the newspapers that Gandhi had arrived in Bombay in connection with important political matters. That evening I took a crowded bus to the distant factory district where the Mahatma lived and held his daily prayer meetings. There was not a palace in India that had not gladly received this old man as a guest, but on his visits to large towns he preferred to live in the slums, in the midst of Indian factory workers and the casteless, because he felt that they were his family.

I stood in this crowd of people, many of whom had never eaten their full, learned to read or write, or been allowed until recently to perform other work than the most menial. Many of them lifted their infants so that they might once in their life see the Mahatma. Millions of poor Hindus did not see in Gandhi the successful politician or the lawyer. They loved him because they felt he was a saint who had entered the political arena out of love for the oppressed people.

Gandhi sat up on a platform on an easy chair, facing the assembled crowd. He looked tired, his hands lay folded on his knees, and his eyes were closed. It happened to be that day of the week when he usually observed silence, so another person read his short speech. But when the loudspeaker sounded, the first words we heard were not those of Gandhi. To my surprise, the mighty resonance of the first lines of the *Isha-Upanishad* rang out in the square framed with factories. The *Isha-Upanishad* is much older than the *Bhagavad-gita*, but for thousands of years the study of the esoteric teaching of the Vedas had been introduced with this Upanishad. Even Shri had observed this when he instructed me. This Upanishad contains the essence of the secrets of the Vedas, which the casteless of India were formerly strictly forbidden to share in. Now it flowed in rhythmical waves over the heads of the untouchables:

> *Isha vasyam idam sarvam*
> *yat kinca jagatyam jagat...*

These lines mean: "May the whole universe, and all that moves in this perishable world, be enveloped in God, the divine Lord." Sanskrit has a fullness and richness that makes it impossible to convey the lines with the conciseness of the original. The words intimate, too, that we should always be conscious that our world is filled with God, invested with God, inhabited by God, permeated by God.

As I stood in the crowd, I thought, this line from the Upanishad is like a threshold. If one understands its meaning, one can live in the midst of the world, with its noise and strife, without being engulfed. Only then can one read the endless path that starts here, leading on into the realm of divine love.

The voice of the Upanishad died away; the crowd, too, was quiet. Up on the platform, one of Gandhi's sons began singing. The verse that he sang was also familiar to me. It was one of God's names, that of divine Rama, that Sadananda and I had often sung together with the happy children on the slope of Himalaya.

Ten times, twenty times, Gandhi's son sang the name Rama. Then he said to the crowd, "Sing with me!" Shyly at first, but gradually louder and full of joy, they sang, all of them sang—latrine cleaners, coolies, street sweepers and workers from the cotton mills. Forty or fifty thousand people sang, and I with them. With raised arms, Gandhi's son set the rhythm. All of us clapped our hands and sang at the top of our voices:

Raghupati Raghava Raja Ram
Patita Pavana Sita Ram

It seemed as if they never wanted to stop singing.

Many of those singing turned hesitatingly, perhaps for the first time, toward God. The old man, who wrote in his memoirs that the name Rama freed him from all fear, sat on the platform listening. No one could have guessed then that a fanatic would shoot the Mahatma just before a similar prayer meeting, silencing the voice that tirelessly insisted that one love one's enemies.

Gandhi had disappeared into the hut where he was living. The crowds stormed the buses, and I realized that I probably was going to have to stand where I was for at least an hour. Then I decided to take one of the nearly empty buses that went far out into the country.

We passed through ugly suburbs, between barracks, factories, gravel heaps, garages, and hangars. I tried to understand what Shri had taught me—that every speck of dust comes from God, and that my own heart has its foundation in him.

When night came, I got off the bus at random and asked a passer-by somewhat anxiously if a street car or bus went in the direction of my hostel. The man laughed. "You do not need to ride. Your hostel is only a couple of hundred steps away," he said. Without knowing it I had returned home.

At the hostel a letter awaited me, the news I had been waiting for. The American Express Company notified me that a sailing reservation had been booked for me. The next morning I began my rounds again to the various government offices. By dinner time I had all the necessary papers and required stamps: permission to leave India, British through-permit, Swedish entrance permit, etc. In my heart, however, I was a little downcast at having to leave India without seeing my friend Sadananda one last time—and without having been initiated.

Dejected and exhausted, I lay down on my bed in the heat of noon, in a room I shared with four old men. Suddenly it seemed to me that I heard Sadananda's voice. He came in with swift strides, tall and slim in his light monk's gown. In the camp he had once said to me: "If you really need me, I shall come to you, even though I am a thousand miles away." And now he had come, to my overwhelming surprise. "Get up, Vamandas," he said. "Hurry up! Time is precious. Put on your best clothes. Swami Bon is waiting in the carriage below."

"We cannot stay here longer than two days, perhaps three," explained Sadananda, as we hurried down the wooden steps of the tall house. "We came only to meet you before your departure for Europe—and Swami Bon will give you the holy name of God and the Indian rosary of Tulasi pearls."

Sadananda's friend sat in the two-wheeled carriage that stood in front of the door. Swami Bon, who had been sent to Europe by his guru, Bhakti-Siddhanta Sarasvati, was the first Bhakta that Sadananda had met. Sadananda had shown me a portrait of Swami Bon's fine features and calm eyes, but he appeared older than I expected. I touched my forehead to his feet by way of greeting and climbed into the carriage. He embraced me heartily. We drove away, disregarding the two men in Indian dress who eyed us suspiciously from the front door of the hostel. They were probably members of the secret police.

We spent only three days together. We walked barefoot through the masses in the courtyard of the great Narayana temple, the seat of Indian orthodoxy. In its halls a pundit expounded the writings in song for a circle of listeners. The three of us sat together on the seashore. We dined together, first offering the food to God as a gift of love, then receiving it again from him as divine grace, partaking it in communion with him.

"Take the spiritual treasure you have found here in India to the West," Sadananda said to me as we said farewell to one another at the central station in Bombay.

The train that my friends were taking left the station. They returned to Brindaban, and I boarded the great ship that was to take me to Europe.

The stately but exceedingly overcrowded luxury steamer seemed unreal, a thing of dreams. Nine of us lay in three layers, one over the other, in a cabin intended for two. During the two-week voyage, the loudspeaker could be heard in every corner of the big ship. The musical program was constantly interrupted by military orders or disciplinary messages. English generals and privates, army chaplains and nurses, even a large group of cabaret artists and uniformed dancers were returning home on this ship. The latter had given performances in the great forests of Assam and Burma, trying to make life a little brighter for the worn-out troops at the front. All day long they lay on the boards of the deck, in short khaki trousers or light bathing-costumes, as if they were at a seaside resort. In the evenings they danced in shimmering evening dresses with the British officers on the festive, brightly lit deck. Everybody's motto seemed to be, "Forget, forget all that has happened!" Meanwhile, nine hundred Italian prisoners of war, taken on at the last minute, camped on a lower, darker deck, tightly crowded. When the Calabrian coast was sighted, these Italians shrieked wildly and rushed to the railing, causing the mighty ship to lurch. The following morning they landed quietly in a devastated Naples, each man carrying his heavy pack on his back.

We traveled on. Impatience and anxiety filled those on board as the ship made record time from Italy around a large part of Europe, past the coasts of Morocco, Spain, Portugal, and France. Then we entered the English Channel, and the waves became grayer. I, too, was impatient, and my heart was filled with a longing for home.

I flew from London, although the ticket was altogether too expensive for my pocket. The fog over England enveloped the airplane so thickly that one could hardly see its wings. For a long while we dived into air pockets, one after another, but when we flew over the North Sea the sun was shining on the granite cliffs of the

Swedish coastal islands. In the roar of the motor I sang aloud, unheard by anyone. I sang the mantra of the name of God, which bestows love, and which surely had never sounded before over this land and these waters. I sang the words with which Krishna Chaitanya, the hidden avatar of the Dark Age, had praised the might of the name of God.

At midnight, holding my worn tropical helmet and breathing the cool, fresh air of the north, I stood on the railway station of a little Swedish town.

A few steps away stood my wife with her head bowed. It seemed as if she had lost hope of my ever returning. Beside her stood a slim thirteen-year-old boy. He had been a little child of four when I had seen him last. He called out in a clear voice: "Father!" and relieved me of my traveling bag. Hella, whom Shri had named Shanti (Peace), looked up and came to me smiling. It seemed as if we had been apart only a few days.

In the room put at my disposal in a hospitable home at the edge of a wood, I began relating my experiences to my wife. All night I sat and spoke beside her bed, and I continued my story over the next few days. Still I felt that I had only reached the beginning of my inexhaustible tale. I saw how my wife blossomed when I told her about the love of God in India, and I sang for her the Bhakti songs that my friend Sadananda had taught me.

"Father, may I listen?" asked my son, who had shyly opened the door of his bedroom and stood barefoot before us.

"Yes. Sit down beside us and listen," said my wife. I continued my song. It was one about Krishna Chaitanya. Outside the open windows, the weeping birches murmured in the light breeze. How amazing! It was the murmur of trees and the earth, no longer the roar of the rivers of Himalaya.